The Provoked Wife

A Comedy

By

John Vanbrugh

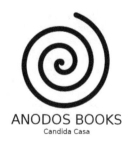

ANODOS BOOKS
Candida Casa

Contents

PROLOGUE.

Spoken by Mrs. *Bracegirdle*.

Since 'tis th' Intent and Business of the Stage,
To copy out the Follies of the Age;
To hold to every Man a faithful Glass,
And shew him of what Species he's an Ass:
I hope the next that teaches in the School,
Will shew our Author he's a scribbling Fool.
And that the Satire may be sure to bite,
Kind Heav'n! inspire some venom'd Priest to write,
And grant some ugly Lady may indite.
For I wou'd have him lash'd, by Heavens! I wou'd,
Till his Presumption swam away in Blood.
Three Plays at once proclaim a Face of Brass,
No matter what they are; That's not the Case—
To write three Plays, e'en that's to be an Ass.
But what I least forgive, he knows it too,
For to his Cost he lately has known you—
Experience shews, to many a Writer's Smart,
You hold a Court where Mercy ne'er had part;
So much of the old Serpent's Sting you have,
You love to Damn, as Heaven delights to Save.
In foreign Parts, let a bold Volunteer,
For Public Good, upon the Stage appear,
He meets ten thousand Smiles to dissipate his Fear.
All tickle on th' adventuring young Beginner,
And only scourge th' incorrigible Sinner;
They touch indeed his Faults, but with a Hand
So gentle, that his Merit still may stand;
Kindly they buoy the Follies of his Pen,
That he may shun 'em when he writes again.
But 'tis not so in this good-natur'd Town,
All's one, an Ox, a Poet, or a Crown;
Old *England's* Play was always knocking down.

DRAMATIS PERSONAE.

MEN.

Constant.

Heartfree.

Sir *John Brute.*

Treble, a Singing-Master.

Rasor, Valet de Chambre to Sir *John Brute.*

Justice of the Peace.

Lord *Rake.*

Col. *Bully.*

WOMEN.

Lady *Brute.*

Belinda, her Niece.

Lady *Fancyfull.*

Madamoiselle.

Cornet and *Pipe,* Servants to Lady *Fancyfull.*

ACT I.

Scene, Sir John Brute's *House.*

Enter Sir John, *solus.*

What cloying Meat is Love—when Matrimony's the Sauce to it! Two Years Marriage has debauch'd my five Senses. Every thing I see, every thing I hear, every thing I feel, every thing I smell, and every thing I taste—methinks has Wife in't. No Boy was ever so weary of his Tutor, no Girl of her Bib, no Nun of doing Penance, or old Maid of being chaste, as I am of being married. Sure there's a secret Curse entail'd upon the very Name of Wife. My Lady is a young Lady, a fine Lady, a witty Lady, a virtuous Lady,—and yet I hate her. There is but one thing on Earth I loath beyond her: That's Fighting. Would my Courage come up to a fourth part of my Ill-Nature, I'd stand buff to her Relations, and thrust her out of doors. But Marriage has sunk me down to such an Ebb of Resolution, I dare not draw my Sword, tho' even to get rid of my Wife. But here she comes.

Enter Lady Brute.

Lady Brute. Do you dine at home to-day, Sir *John?*

Sir John. Why, do you expect I should tell you what I don't know myself?

Lady Brute. I thought there was no harm in asking you.

Sir John. If thinking wrong were an excuse for Impertinence, Women might be justify'd in most things they say or do.

Lady Brute. I'm sorry I have said any thing to displease you.

Sir John. Sorrow for things past is of as little importance to me, as my dining at home or abroad ought to be to you.

Lady Brute. My Enquiry was only that I might have provided what you lik'd.

Sir John. Six to four you had been in the wrong there again; for what I lik'd yesterday I don't like to-day; and what I like to-day, 'tis odds I mayn't like to-morrow.

Lady Brute. But if I had ask'd you what you lik'd?

Sir John. Why then there wou'd have been more asking about it than the thing was worth.

Lady Brute. I wish I did but know how I might please you.

Sir John. Ay, but that sort of Knowledge is not a Wife's Talent.

Lady Brute. Whate'er my Talent is, I'm sure my Will has ever been to make you easy.

Sir John. If Women were to have their Wills, the World wou'd be finely govern'd.

Lady Brute. What reason have I given you to use me as you do of late? It once was otherwise: You marry'd me for Love.

Sir John. And you me for Money: So you have your Reward, and I have mine.

Lady Brute. What is it that disturbs you?

Sir John. A Parson.

Lady Brute. Why, what has he done to you?

Sir John. He has married me.

[*Exit Sir John.*

Lady Brute, *sola.*

The Devil's in the Fellow, I think——I was told before I married him, that thus 'twou'd be: But I thought I had Charms enough to govern him; and that where there was an Estate, a Woman must needs be happy; so my Vanity has deceiv'd me, and my Ambition has made me uneasy. But there's some Comfort still; if one wou'd be reveng'd of him, these are good times; a Woman may have a Gallant, and a separate Maintenance too—The surly Puppy—yet he's a Fool for't: for hitherto he has been no Monster: But who knows how far he may provoke me? I never lov'd him, yet I have been ever true to him; and that, in spite of all the Attacks of Art and Nature upon a poor weak Woman's Heart, in favour of a tempting Lover. Methinks so noble a Defence as I have made, shou'd be rewarded with a better Usage—Or who can tell?——Perhaps a good part of what I suffer from my Husband, may be a Judgment upon me for my Cruelty to my Lover.——Lord, with what pleasure could I indulge that Thought, were there but a Possibility of

6

finding Arguments to make it good!——-And how do I know but there may?—Let me see——What opposes?—My matrimonial Vow—— Why, what did I vow? I think I promis'd to be true to my Husband. Well; and he promis'd to be kind to me. But he han't kept his Word ——Why then I'm absolv'd from mine—Ay, that seems clear to me. The Argument's good between the King and the People, why not between the Husband and the Wife? O, but that Condition was not exprest—No matter, 'twas understood. Well, by all I see, if I argue the matter a little longer with myself, I shan't find so many Bug-bears in the Way as I thought I shou'd. Lord, what fine Notions of Virtue do we Women take up upon the Credit of old foolish Philosophers! Virtue's its own Reward, Virtue's this, Virtue's that——Virtue's an Ass, and a Gallant's worth forty on't.

Enter Belinda.

Lady Brute. Good-morrow, dear Cousin.

Bel. Good-morrow, Madam; you look pleas'd this Morning.

Lady Brute. I am so.

Bel. With what, pray?

Lady Brute. With my Husband.

Bel. Drown Husbands; for your's is a provoking Fellow: As he went out just now, I pray'd him to tell me what time of Day 'twas; and he ask'd me if I took him for the Church-Clock, that was oblig'd to tell all the Parish.

Lady Brute. He has been saying some good obliging things to me too. In short, *Belinda*, he has us'd me so barbarously of late, that I cou'd almost resolve to play the downright Wife—and cuckold him.

Bel. That would be downright indeed.

Lady Brute. Why, after all, there's more to be said for't than you'd imagine, Child. I know, according to the strict Statute-Law of Religion, I shou'd do wrong: But if there were a Court of Chancery in Heav'n, I'm sure I shou'd cast him.

Bel. If there were a House of Lords, you might.

Lady Brute. In either I should infallibly carry my Cause. Why, he is the first Aggressor, not I.

Bel. Ay, but you know we must return Good for Evil.

Lady Brute. That may be a Mistake in the Translation—Pr'ythee be of my Opinion, *Belinda*; for I'm positive I'm in the right; and if you'll keep up the Prerogative of a Woman, you'll likewise be positive you are in the right, whenever you do any thing you have a mind to. But I shall play the Fool, and jest on, till I make you begin to think I'm in earnest.

Bel. I shan't take the Liberty, Madam, to think of any thing that you desire to keep a Secret from me.

Lady Brute. Alas, my Dear, I have no Secrets. My Heart cou'd never yet confine my Tongue.

Bel. Your Eyes, you mean; for I'm sure I have seen them gadding, when your Tongue has been lock'd up safe enough.

Lady Brute. My Eyes gadding! Pr'ythee after who, Child?

Bel. Why, after one that thinks you hate him, as much as I know you love him.

Lady Brute. Constant you mean.

Bel. I do so.

Lady Brute. Lord, what shou'd put such a thing into your Head?

Bel. That which puts things into most People's Heads, Observation.

Lady Brute. Why what have you observ'd, in the Name of Wonder?

Bel. I have observed you blush when you met him; force yourself away from him; and then be out of humour with every thing about you: In a Word, never was poor Creature so spurr'd on by Desire, and so rein'd in with Fear.

Lady Brute. How strong is Fancy!

Bel. How weak is Woman!

Lady Brute. Pr'ythee, Niece, have a better Opinion of your Aunt's Inclination.

Bel. Dear Aunt, have a better Opinion of your Niece's Understanding.

Lady Brute. You'll make me angry.

8

Bel. You'll make me laugh.

Lady Brute. Then you are resolv'd to persist?

Bel. Positively.

Lady Brute. And all I can say——

Bel. Will signify nothing.

Lady Brute. Tho' I should swear 'twere false—

Bel. I should think it true.

Lady Brute. Then let us both forgive; [*Kissing her.*] for we have both offended: I, in making a Secret; you, in discovering it.

Bel. Good Nature may do much: But you have more Reason to forgive one, than I have to pardon t'other.

Lady Brute. 'Tis true, *Belinda*, you have given me so many Proofs of your Friendship, that my Reserve has been indeed a Crime: But that you may more easily forgive me, remember, Child, that when our Nature prompts us to a thing our Honour and Religion have forbid us; we wou'd (wer't possible) conceal even from the Soul itself, the Knowledge of the Body's Weakness.

Bel. Well, I hope, to make your Friend amends, you'll hide nothing from her for the future, tho' the Body shou'd still grow weaker and weaker.

Lady Brute. No, from this Moment I have no more Reserve; and for a Proof of my Repentance, I own, *Belinda*, I'm in danger. Merit and Wit assault me from without; Nature and Love sollicit me within; my Husband's barbarous Usage piques me to Revenge; and *Satan*, catching at the fair Occasion, throws in my way that Vengeance, which of all Vengeance pleases Women best.

Bel. 'Tis well *Constant* don't know the Weakness of the Fortification; for o' my Conscience he'd soon come on to the Assault.

Lady Brute. Ay, and I'm afraid carry the Town too. But whatever you may have observ'd, I have dissembled so well as to keep him ignorant. So you see I'm no Coquette, *Belinda:* And if you follow my Advice, you'll never be one neither. 'Tis true, Coquetry is one of the main Ingredients in the natural Composition of a Woman; and I, as well as

9

others, cou'd be well enough pleas'd to see a Crowd of young Fellows ogling, and glancing, and watching all Occasions to do forty foolish officious Things: Nay, shou'd some of 'em push on, even to hanging or drowning, why—'faith—if I shou'd let pure Woman alone, I shou'd e'en be but too well pleas'd with it.

Bel. I'll swear 'twould tickle me strangely.

Lady Brute. But after all, 'tis a vicious Practice in us, to give the least Encouragement but where we design to come to a Conclusion. For 'tis an unreasonable thing to engage a Man in a Disease, which we beforehand resolve we never will apply a Cure to.

Bel. 'Tis true; but then a Woman must abandon one of the supreme Blessings of her Life. For I am fully convinc'd, no Man has half that Pleasure in possessing a Mistress, as a Woman has in jilting a Gallant.

Lady Brute. The happiest Woman then on Earth must be our Neighbour.

Bel. O the impertinent Composition! She has Vanity and Affectation enough to make her a ridiculous Original, in spite of all that Art and Nature ever furnish'd to any of her Sex before her.

Lady Brute. She concludes all Men her Captives; and whatever Course they take, it serves to confirm her in that Opinion.

Bel. If they shun her, she thinks 'tis Modesty, and takes it for a Proof of their Passion.

Lady Brute. And if they are rude to her, 'tis Conduct, and done to prevent Town-talk.

Bel. When her Folly makes 'em laugh; she thinks they are pleased with her Wit.

Lady Brute. And when her Impertinence makes 'em dull, concludes they are jealous of her Favours.

Bel. All their Actions and their Words, she takes for granted, aim at her.

Lady Brute. And pities all other Women, because she thinks they envy her.

Bel. Pray, out of pity to ourselves, let us find a better Subject; for I'm weary of this. Do you think your Husband inclined to Jealousy?

Lady Brute. O, no; he does not love me well enough for that. Lord, how wrong Men's Maxims are! They are seldom jealous of their Wives, unless they are very fond of 'em; whereas they ought to consider the Women's Inclinations; for there depends their Fate. Well, Men may talk; But they are not so wise as we——that's certain.

Bel. At least in our Affairs.

Lady Brute. Nay, I believe we shou'd out-do 'em in the Business of the State too: For, methinks, they do and undo, and make but bad Work on't.

Bel. Why then don't we get into the Intrigues of Government as well as they?

Lady Brute. Because we have Intrigues of our own, that make us more Sport, Child. And so let's in and consider of 'em.

[*Exeunt.*

Scene, A Dressing-Room.

Enter Lady Fancyfull, Madamoiselle, *and* Cornet.

Lady Fan. How do I look this Morning?

Cor. Your Ladyship looks very ill, truly.

Lady Fan. Lard, how ill-natur'd thou art, Cornet, to tell me so, tho' the thing shou'd be true! Don't you know that I have Humility enough to be but too easily out of Conceit with myself? Hold the Glass; I dare swear that will have more Manners than you have. *Madamoiselle,* let me have your Opinion too.

Madam. My opinion pe, Matam, dat your Latyship never look so well in your Life.

Lady Fan. Well, the *French* are the prettiest, obliging People; they say the most acceptable, well-manner'd things—and never flatter.

Madam. Your Latyship say great Justice inteed.

Lady Fan. Nay, every thing's just in my House but *Cornet.* The very Looking-Glass gives her the *Dementi.* But I'm almost afraid it flatters me, it makes me look so very engaging.

[*Looking affectedly in the Glass.*

11

Madam. Inteed, Matam, your face pe handsomer den all de Looking-Glass in de World, *croyez moy.*

Lady Fan. But is it possible my Eyes can be so languishing—and so very full of Fire?

Madam. Matam, if de Glass was Burning-Glass, I believe your Eyes set de Fire in de House.

Lady Fan. You may take that Night-gown, *Madamoiselle;* get out of the Room, *Cornet;* I can't endure you. This Wench, methinks, does look so unsufferably ugly.

Madam. Every ting look ugly, Matam, dat stand by your Latyship.

Lady Fan. No really, *Madamoiselle,* methinks you look mighty pretty.

Madam. Ah Matam! de Moon have no Eclat ven de Sun appear.

Lady Fan. O pretty Expression! Have you ever been in Love, *Madamoiselle?*

Madam. Ouy, Matame.

[*Sighing.*

Lady Fan. And were you belov'd again?

Madam. Non, Matame.

Lady Fan. O ye Gods! What an unfortunate Creature shou'd I be in such a Case! But Nature has made me nice, for my own Defence: I'm nice, strangely nice, *Madamoiselle;* I believe were the Merit of whole Mankind bestow'd upon one single Person, I shou'd still think the Fellow wanted something to make it worth my while to take notice of him; and yet I could love; nay, fondly love, were it possible to have a thing made on purpose for me: For I'm not cruel, *Madamoiselle;* I'm only nice.

Madam. Ah Matam, I wish I was fine Gentleman for your sake. I do all de ting in de World to get leetel way into your Heart. I make Song, I make Verse, I give you de Serenade, I give great many Present to *Madamoiselle;* I no eat, I no sleep, I be lean, I be mad, I hang myself, I drown myself. *Ah ma chere Dame, que je vous aimerois!*

[*Embracing her.*

Lady Fan. Well, the *French* have strange obliging ways with 'em; you may take those two pair of Gloves, Madamoiselle.

Madam. Me humbly tanke my sweet Lady.

Enter Cornet.

Cor. Madam, here's a Letter for your Ladyship by the Penny Post.

Lady Fan. Some new Conquest, I'll warrant you. For without Vanity, I look'd extremely clear last Night when I went to the Park.—O agreeable! Here's a new Song made of me: And ready set too. O thou welcome thing! [*Kissing it.*] Call *Pipe* hither, she shall sing it instantly.

Enter Pipe.

Here, sing me this new Song, *Pipe.*

Song.

I.

Fly, fly, you happy Shepherds, fly;
Avoid Philira's Charms;
The Rigour of her Heart denies
The Heaven that's in her Arms.
Ne'er hope to gaze, and then retire,
Nor yielding, to be blest;
Nature, who form'd her Eyes of Fire,
Of ice compos'd her Breast.

II.

Yet, lovely Maid, this once believed
A Slave whose Zeal you move;
The Gods, alas! your Youth deceive,
Their Heav'n consists in Love.
In spite of all the Thanks you owe,
You may reproach 'em this;
That where they did their Form bestow,
They have deny'd their Bliss.

Lady Fan. Well, there may be Faults, *Madamoiselle*, but the Design is so very obliging, 'twou'd be a matchless Ingratitude in me to discover 'em.

Madam. Ma foy, Madame, I tink de Gentleman's Song tell you de

13

Trute. If you never love, you never be happy—Ah—*que l'aime l'amour moy!*

Enter Servant *with another letter.*

Ser. Madam, here's another Letter for your Ladyship.

Lady Fan. 'Tis this way I am importun'd every Morning, *Madamoiselle.* Pray how do the *French* Ladies when they are thus *accablées?*

Madam. Matam, dey never complain. *Au contraire,* when one *Frense* Laty have got hundred Lover—den she do all she can—to get a hundred more.

Lady Fan. Well, strike me dead, I think they have *le Gout bon.* For 'tis an unutterable Pleasure to be ador'd by all the Men, and envy'd by all the Women——Yet I'll swear I'm concern'd at the Torture I give 'em. Lard, why was I form'd to make the whole Creation uneasy! But let me read my Letter. [*Reads.*]

"If you have a mind to hear of your Faults, instead of being prais'd for your Virtues, take the pains to walk in the Green-walk in St. *James's* with your Woman an Hour hence. You'll there meet one, who hates you for some things, as he cou'd love you for others, and therefore is willing to endeavour your Reformation.——If you come to the Place I mention, you'll know who I am: If you don't, you never shall: so take your Choice."

This is strangely familiar, *Madamoiselle;* now have I a provoking Fancy to know who this impudent Fellow is.

Madam. Den take your Scarf and your Mask, and go to de Rendezvous. De *Frense* Laty do *justement comme ça.*

Lady Fan. Rendezvous! What, rendezvous with a Man, *Madamoiselle!*

Madam. Eh, pourquoy non?

Lady Fan. What, and a Man perhaps I never saw in my Life?

Madam. Tant mieux: c'est donc quelque chose de nouveau.

Lady Fan. Why, how do I know what Designs he may have? He may intend to ravish me, for aught I know.

Madam. Ravish!—Bagatelle. I would fain see one impudent Rogue ravish *Madamoiselle: Ouy, je le voudrois.*

14

Lady Fan. O, but my Reputation, Madamoiselle! my Reputation! *Ah ma chere* Reputation!

Madam. Madame—*Quand on la une fois perdue—On n'en est plus embarassée.*

Lady Fan. Fe, *Madamoiselle,* Fe! Reputation is a Jewel.

Madam. Qui coute bien chere, Madame.

Lady Fan. Why sure you would not sacrifice your Honour to your Pleasure?

Madam. Je suis Philosophe.

Lady Fan. Bless me, how you talk! Why, what if Honour be a Burden, *Madamoiselle,* must it not be borne?

Madam. Chaqu'un a sa façon—Quand quelque chose m'incommode moy —je m'en defais vite.

Lady Fan. Get you gone, you little naughty *French*-woman, you; I vow and swear I must turn you out of doors, if you talk thus.

Madam. Turn me out of doors!—--Turn yourself out of doors, and go see what de Gentleman have to say to you—*Tenez. Voila* [*Giving her her things hastily.*] *vostre Esharpe, voila vostre Quoife, voila vostre Masque, voila tout* Hey, *Mercure, Coquin:* Call one Chair for Matam, and one oder [*Calling within.*] for me: *Va t'en vite.* [*Turning to her Lady, and helping her on hastily with her things.*] *Allons, Madame, depechez vous donc. Mon Dieu, quelles Scrupules!*

Lady Fan. Well, for once, *Madamoiselle,* I'll follow your Advice, out of the intemperate Desire I have to know who this ill-bred Fellow is. But I have too much *Delicatesse,* to make a Practice on't.

Madam. Belle chose vrayment que la Delicatesse, lors qu'il s'agit de se devertir—à ça—Vous voila equipés, partons.—He bien!—qu'avez vous donc?

Lady Fan. J'ay peur.

Madam. Je n'en ay point moy.

Lady Fan. I dare not go.

Madam. Demeurez donc.

Lady Fan. Je suis poltrone.

Madam. Tant pis pour vous.

Lady Fan. Curiosity's a wicked Devil.

Madam. C'est une charmante Sainte.

Lady Fan. It ruined our first Parents.

Madam. Elle a bien diverti leurs Enfans.

Lady Fan. L'Honneur est contre.

Madam. La Plaisir est pour.

Lady Fan. Must I then go?

Madam. Must you go?—Must you eat, must you drink, must you sleep, must you live? De Nature bid you do one, de Nature bid you do toder. *Vous me ferez enrager.*

Lady Fan. But when Reason corrects Nature, *Madamoiselle——*

Madam. Elle est donc bien insolente, c'est sa Sœur aisnée.

Lady Fan. Do you then prefer your Nature to your Reason, *Madamoiselle?*

Madam. Ouy da.

Lady Fan. Pourquoy?

Madam. Because my Nature make me merry, my Reason make me mad.

Lady Fan. Ah la mechante Françoise!

Madam. Ah la belle Angloise!

[*Forcing her Lady off.*

16

ACT II.

Scene, St. James's Park.

Enter Lady Fancyfull *and* Madamoiselle.

Lady Fan. Well, I vow, *Madamoiselle,* I'm strangely impatient to know who this confident Fellow is.

Enter Heartfree.

Look, there's *Heartfree.* But sure it can't be him; he's a profess'd Woman-hater. Yet who knows what my wicked Eyes may have done?

Madam. Il nous approche, Madame.

Lady Fan. Yes, 'tis he: now will he be most intolerably cavalier, tho' he should be in love with me.

Heart. Madam, I'm your humble Servant; I perceive you have more Humility and Good-Nature than I thought you had.

Lady Fan. What you attribute to Humility and Good-Nature, Sir, may perhaps be only due to Curiosity. I had a mind to know who 'twas had ill manners enough to write that Letter.

[*Throwing him his Letter.*

Heart. Well, and now I hope you are satisfy'd.

Lady Fan. I am so, Sir: Good by t'ye.

Heart. Nay, hold there; tho' you have done your Business, I han't done mine: By your Ladyship's leave, we must have one Moment's Prattle together. Have you a mind to be the prettiest Woman about Town, or not? How she stares upon me! What! this passes for an impertinent Question with you now, because you think you are so already?

Lady Fan. Pray, Sir, let me ask you a Question in my Turn: By what Right do you pretend to examine me?

Heart. By the same Right that the strong govern the weak, because I have you in my power; for you cannot get so quickly to your Coach, but I shall have time enough to make you hear every thing I have to say to you.

Lady Fan. These are strange Liberties you take, Mr. *Heartfree.*

Heart. They are so, Madam, but there's no help for it; for know that I have a Design upon you.

Lady Fan. Upon me, Sir!

Heart. Yes; and one that will turn to your Glory, and my Comfort, if you will but be a little wiser than you use to be.

Lady Fan. Very well, Sir.

Heart. Let me see——Your Vanity, Madam, I take to be about some eight Degrees higher than any Woman's in the Town, let t'other be who she will; and my Indifference is naturally about the same Pitch. Now, could you find the way to turn this Indifference into Fire and Flames, methinks your Vanity ought to be satisfy'd; and this, perhaps, you might bring about upon pretty reasonable Terms.

Lady Fan. And pray at what rate would this Indifference be bought off, if one shou'd have so depraved an Appetite to desire it?

Heart. Why, Madam, to drive a Quaker's Bargain, and make but one word with you, if I do part with it—you must lay me down—your Affectation.

Lady Fan. My Affectation, Sir!

Heart. Why, I ask you nothing but what you may very well spare.

Lady Fan. You grow rude, Sir. Come, *Madamoiselle*, 'tis high time to be gone.

Madam. Allons, allons, allons.

Heart. [*Stopping them.*] Nay, you may as well stand still; for hear me you shall, walk which way you please.

Lady Fan. What mean you, Sir?

Heart. I mean to tell you, that you are the most ungrateful Woman upon Earth.

Lady Fan. Ungrateful! To whom?

Heart. To Nature.

Lady Fan. Why, what has Nature done for me?

Heart. What you have undone by Art! It made you handsome; it gave you Beauty to a Miracle, a Shape without a Fault, Wit enough to make them relish, and so turn'd you loose to your own Discretion; which has made such work with you, that you are become the Pity of our Sex, and the Jest of your own. There is not a Feature in your Face, but you have found the way to teach it some affected Convulsion; your Feet, your Hands, your very Fingers Ends are directed never to move without some ridiculous Air or other; and your Language is a suitable Trumpet, to draw people's Eyes upon the Raree-show.

Madam. [*Aside.*] *Est ce qu'on fait l'amour en Angleterre comme ça?*

Lady Fan. [*Aside.*] Now cou'd I cry for Madness, but that I know he'd laugh at me for it.

Heart. Now do you hate me for telling you the Truth, but that's because you don't believe it is so; for were you once convinc'd of that, you'd reform for your own sake. But 'tis as hard to persuade a Woman to quit any thing that makes her ridiculous, as 'tis to prevail with a Poet to see a Fault in his own Play.

Lady Fan. Every Circumstance of nice Breeding must needs appear ridiculous to one who has so natural an Antipathy to Good-manners.

Heart. But suppose I could find the means to convince you, that the whole World is of my Opinion, and that those who flatter and commend you, do it to no other Intent, but to make you persevere in your Folly, that they may continue in their Mirth.

Lady Fan. Sir, tho' you and all that World you talk of shou'd be so impertinently officious, as to think to persuade me I don't know how to behave myself; I shou'd still have Charity enough for my own Understanding, to believe myself in the right, and all you in the wrong.

Madam. Le voila mort.

[*Exeunt Lady Fancyfull and Madamoiselle.*

Heart. [*Gazing after her.*] There her single Clapper has publish'd the Sense of the whole Sex. Well, this once I have endeavour'd to wash the Blackamoor white, but henceforward I'll sooner undertake to teach Sincerity to a Courtier, Generosity to an Usurer, Honesty to a Lawyer, nay, Humility to a Divine, than Discretion to a Woman I see has once set her Heart upon playing the Fool.

Enter Constant.

19

'Morrow, *Constant.*

Const. Good-morrow, *Jack!* What are you doing here this Morning?

Heart. Doing! Guess, if thou canst.——Why I have been endeavouring to persuade my Lady *Fancyfull,* that she's the foolishest Woman about Town.

Const. A pretty Endeavour, truly!

Heart. I have told her in as plain *English* as I could speak, both what the Town says of her, and what I think of her. In short, I have us'd her as an absolute King would do *Magna Charta.*

Const. And how does she take it?

Heart. As Children do Pills; bite them, but can't swallow them.

Const. But, pr'ythee, what has put it into your Head, of all Mankind, to turn Reformer?

Heart. Why one thing was, the Morning hung upon my Hands, I did not know what to do with myself; and another was, that as little as I care for Women, I cou'd not see with Patience one that Heaven had taken such wondrous Pains about, be so very industrious to make herself the Jack-pudding of the Creation.

Const. Well, now could I almost wish to see my cruel Mistress make the self-same Use of what Heaven has done for her, that so I might be cur'd of a Disease that makes me so very uneasy; for Love, Love is the Devil, *Heartfree.*

Heart. And why do you let the Devil govern you?

Const. Because I have more Flesh and Blood than Grace and Self-denial. My dear, dear Mistress! 'S death! that so genteel a Woman should be a Saint, when Religion's out of Fashion!

Heart. Nay, she's much in the wrong, truly; but who knows how far Time and good Example may prevail?

Const. O! they have play'd their Parts in vain already: 'Tis now two Years since that damned Fellow her Husband invited me to his Wedding; and there was the first time I saw that charming Woman, whom I have lov'd ever since, more than e'er a Martyr did his Soul; but she is cold, my Friend, still cold as the Northern Star.

Heart. So are all Women by Nature, which makes them so willing to be warm'd.

Const. O don't prophane the Sex! Pr'ythee, think them all Angels for her sake; for she's virtuous even to a Fault.

Heart. A Lover's Head is a good accountable Thing truly; he adores his Mistress for being virtuous, and yet is very angry with her because she won't be lewd.

Const. Well, the only Relief I expect in my Misery, is to see thee some Day or other as deeply engag'd as myself, which will force me to be merry in the midst of all my Misfortunes.

Heart. That Day will never come, be assur'd, *Ned.* Not but that I can pass a Night with a Woman, and for the time, perhaps; make myself as good Sport as you can do. Nay, I can court a Woman too, call her Nymph, Angel, Goddess, what you please: But here's the Difference 'twixt you and I; I persuade a Woman she's an Angel, and she persuades you she's one. Pr'ythee, let me tell you how I avoid falling in Love; that which serves me for Prevention, may chance to serve you for a Cure.

Const. Well, use the Ladies moderately then, and I'll hear you.

Heart. That using them moderately undoes us all; but I'll use them justly, and that you ought to be satisfied with. I always consider a Woman, not as the Taylor, the Shoemaker, the Tire-woman, the Sempstress, and (which is more than all that) the Poet makes her; but I consider her as pure Nature has contrived her, and that more strictly than I shou'd have done our old Grandmother *Eve,* had I seen her naked in the Garden; for I consider her turn'd inside out. Her Heart well examin'd, I find there Pride, Vanity, Covetousness, Indiscretion, but above all things, Malice; plots eternally a-forging to destroy one another's Reputations, and as honestly to charge the Levity of Men's Tongues with the Scandal; hourly Debates how to make poor Gentlemen in love with them, with no other Intent but to use them like Dogs when they have done; a constant Desire of doing more Mischief, and an everlasting War wag'd against Truth and Good-Nature.

Const. Very well, Sir! An admirable Composition, truly!

Heart. Then for her Outside, I consider it merely as an Outside; she has a thin Tiffany Covering over just such Stuff as you and I are made on. As for her Motion, her Mien, her Airs, and all those Tricks, I know they affect you mightily. If you should see your Mistress at a Coronation dragging her Peacock's Train, with all her State and Insolence about her, 'twou'd strike you with all the awful Thoughts that Heav'n itself could pretend to from you; whereas I turn the whole Matter into a Jest, and suppose her strutting in the self-same stately Manner, with nothing on her but her Stays and her under scanty quilted Petticoat.

Const. Hold thy profane Tongue; for I'll hear no more.

Heart. What, you'll love on, then?

Const. Yes, to Eternity.

Heart. Yet you have no hopes at all?

Const. None.

Heart. Nay, the Resolution may be discreet enough; perhaps you have found out some new Philosophy, that Love, like Virtue, is its own Reward: So you and your Mistress will be as well content at a Distance, as others that have less Learning are in coming together.

Const. No; but if she should prove kind at last, my dear *Heartfree—*

[*Embracing him.*

Heart. Nay, pr'ythee, don't take me for your Mistress; for Lovers are very troublesome.

Const. Well; who knows what Time may do?

Heart. And just now he was sure Time could do nothing.

Const. Yet not one kind Glance in two Years, is somewhat strange.

Heart. Not strange at all; she don't like you, that's all the Business.

Const. Pr'ythee, don't distract me.

Heart. Nay, you are a good handsome young Fellow, she might use you better: Come, will you go see her? Perhaps she may have chang'd her Mind; there's some Hopes as long as she's a Woman.

Const. O, 'tis in vain to visit her! Sometimes to get a Sight of her, I visit that Beast her Husband; but she certainly finds some Pretence to quit the Room as soon as I enter.

Heart. 'Tis much she don't tell him you have made Love to her too; for

22

that's another good-natur'd thing usual amongst Women, in which they have several Ends. Sometimes 'tis to recommend their Virtue, that they may be lewd with the greater Security. Sometimes 'tis to make their Husbands fight, in hopes they may be kill'd, when their Affairs require it should be so: but most commonly 'tis to engage two Men in a Quarrel, that they may have the Credit of being fought for; and if the Lover's kill'd in the Business, they cry, *Poor Fellow*, he had ill Luck——and so they go to Cards.

Const. Thy Injuries to Women are not to be forgiven. Look to't, if ever thou dost fall into their Hands——

Heart. They can't use me worse than they do you, that speak well of 'em. O ho! here comes the Knight.

Enter Sir John Brute.

Heart. Your humble Servant, Sir *John.*

Sir John. Servant, Sir.

Heart. How does all your Family?

Sir John. Pox o' my Family!

Const. How does your Lady? I han't seen her abroad a good while.

Sir John. Do! I don't know how she does, not I; she was well enough Yesterday; I han't been at home to-night.

Const. What, were you out of Town?

Sir John. Out of Town! No, I was drinking.

Const. You are a true *Englishman;* don't know your own Happiness. If I were married to such a Woman, I would not be from her a Night for all the Wine in *France.*

Sir John. Not from her!——'Oons——what a time should a Man have of that!

Heart. Why, there's no Division, I hope.

Sir John. No; but there's a Conjunction, and that's worse; a Pox of the Parson——Why the plague don't you two marry? I fancy I look like the Devil to you.

Heart. Why, you don't think you have Horns, do you?

Sir John. No, I believe my Wife's Religion will keep her honest.

Heart. And what will make her keep her Religion?

Sir John. Persecution; and therefore she shall have it.

Heart. Have a care, Knight! Women are tender things.

Sir John. And yet, methinks, 'tis a hard Matter to break their Hearts.

Const. Fy, fy! You have one of the best Wives in the World, and yet you seem the most uneasy Husband.

Sir John. Best Wives! The Woman's well enough; she has no Vice that I know of, but she's a Wife, and—damn a Wife! If I were married to a Hogshead of Claret, Matrimony would make me hate it.

Heart. Why did you marry, then? You were old enough to know your own Mind.

Sir John. Why did I marry? I married because I had a mind to lie with her, and she would not let me.

Heart. Why did you not ravish her?

Sir John. Yes, and so have hedg'd myself into forty Quarrels with her Relations, besides buying my pardon: But more than all that, you must know, I was afraid of being damn'd in those days: For I kept sneaking, cowardly Company, Fellows that went to Church, said Grace to their Meat, and had not the least Tincture of Quality about them.

Heart. But I think you are got into a better Gang now?

Sir John. Zoons, Sir, my Lord *Rake* and I are Hand and Glove: I believe we may get our Bones broke together to-night; have you a mind to share a Frolick?

Const. Not I, truly; my Talent lies to softer Exercises.

Sir John. What, a Down-Bed and a Strumpet? A pox of Venery, I say. Will you come and drink with me this Afternoon?

Const. I can't drink to-day, but we'll come and sit an Hour with you, if you will.

Sir John. Phugh, Pox, sit an Hour! Why can't you drink?

Const. Because I'm to see my Mistress.

Sir John. Who's that?

Const. Why, do you use to tell?

Sir John. Yes.

Const. So won't I.

Sir John. Why?

Const. Because 'tis a Secret.

Sir John. Would my Wife knew it, 'twould be no Secret long.

Const. Why, do you think she can't keep a Secret?

Sir John. No more than she can keep *Lent*.

Heart. Pr'ythee, tell it her to try, Constant.

Sir John. No, pr'ythee, don't, that I mayn't be plagu'd with it.

Const. I'll hold you a Guinea you don't make her tell it you.

Sir John. I'll hold you a Guinea I do.

Const. Which way?

Sir John. Why, I'll beg her not to tell it me.

Heart. Nay, if any thing does it, that will.

Const. But do you think, Sir——

Sir John. Oons, Sir, I think a Woman and a Secret are the two impertinentest Themes in the Universe: Therefore pray let's hear no more of my Wife, nor your Mistress. Damn 'em both with all my heart, and every thing else that daggles a Petticoat, except four generous Whores, with *Betty Sands* at the Head of 'em, who are drunk with my Lord *Rake* and I ten times in a Fortnight.

[*Exit Sir John.*

Const. Here's a dainty Fellow for you! And the veriest Coward too. But his Usage of his Wife makes me ready to stab the Villain.

Heart. Lovers are short-sighted: All their Senses run into that of Feeling.

25

This Proceeding of his is the only thing on Earth can make your Fortune. If any thing can prevail with her to accept of a Gallant, 'tis his ill Usage of her; for Women will do more for Revenge, than they'll do for the Gospel. Pr'ythee, take heart, I have great hopes for you: And since I can't bring you quite off of her, I'll endeavour to bring you quite on; for a whining Lover is the damn'dest Companion upon Earth.

Const. My dear Friend, flatter me a little more with these Hopes; for whilst they prevail, I have Heaven within me, and could melt with Joy.

Heart. Pray, no melting yet; let things go farther first. This afternoon, perhaps, we shall make some advance. In the mean while, let's go dine at *Locket's*, and let Hope get you a Stomach.

[*Exeunt.*

Scene, Lady Fancyfull's *House.*

Enter Lady Fancyfull *and* Madamoiselle.

Lady Fan. Did you ever see any thing so *importune, Madamoiselle?*

Madam. Inteed, Matam, to say de trute, he want leetel Good-breeding.

Lady Fan. Good-breeding! He wants to be caned, *Madamoiselle:* an insolent Fellow! And yet let me expose my Weakness, 'tis the only Man on Earth I cou'd resolve to dispense my Favours on, were he but a fine Gentleman. Well! did Men but know how deep an Impression a fine Gentleman makes in a Lady's Heart, they would reduce all their Studies to that of Good-breeding alone.

Enter Cornet.

Cor. Madam, here's Mr. *Treble.* He has brought home the Verses your Ladyship made, and gave him to set.

Lady Fan. O let him come in by all means. Now *Madamoiselle,* am I going to be unspeakably happy.

Enter Treble.

So, Mr. *Treble,* you have set my little Dialogue?

Treb. Yes, Madam, and I hope your Ladyship will be pleased with it.

Lady Fan. O, no doubt on't; for really, Mr. *Treble,* you set all things to a wonder: But your Musick is in particular heavenly, when you have my

Words to clothe in't.

Treb. Your Words themselves, Madam, have so much Musick in 'em, they inspire me.

Lady Fan. Nay, now you make me blush, Mr. *Treble;* but pray let's hear what you have done.

Treb. You shall, Madam.

A *Song*, to be sung between a Man and a Woman.

M. *Ah lovely Nymph, the World's on fire;*
Veil, veil those cruel Eyes:

W. *The World may then in Flames expire,*
And boast that so it dies.

M. *But when all Mortals are destroy'd,*
Who then shall sing your Praise?

W. *Those who are fit to be employ'd:*
The Gods shall Altars raise.

Treb. How does your Ladyship like it, Madam?

Lady Fan. Rapture, Rapture, Mr. *Treble!* I'm all Rapture! O Wit and Art, what Power have you when join'd! I must needs tell you the Birth of this little Dialogue, Mr. *Treble.* Its Father was a Dream, and its Mother was the Moon. I dream'd that by an unanimous Vote, I was chosen Queen of that pale World; and that the first time I appear'd upon my Throne——all my Subjects fell in love with me. Just then I wak'd, and seeing Pen, Ink and Paper lie idle upon the Table, I slid into my Morning-Gown, and writ this *impromptu.*

Treb. So I guess the Dialogue, Madam, is suppos'd to be between your Majesty and your first Minister of State.

Lady Fan. Just: He, as Minister, advises me to trouble my Head about the Welfare of my Subjects; which I, as Sovereign, find a very impertinent Proposal. But is the Town so dull, Mr. *Treble,* it affords us never another new Song?

Treb. Madam, I have one in my Pocket, came out but Yesterday, if your Ladyship pleases to let Mrs. *Pipe* sing it.

Lady Fan. By all means. Here, *Pipe,* make what Musick you can of this

Song, here.

SONG.

I.

Not an Angel Dwells above,
Half so fair as her I love.
Heaven knows, how she'll receive me;
If she smiles, I'm blest indeed;
If she frowns, I'm quickly freed;
Heaven knows she ne'er can grieve me.

II.

None can love her more than I,
Yet she ne'er shall make me die.
If my Flame can never warm her,
Lasting Beauty I'll adore;
I shall never love her more,
Cruelty will so deform her.

Lady Fan. Very well: This is *Heartfree's* Poetry without question.

Treb. Won't your Ladyship please to sing yourself this Morning?

Lady Fan. O Lord, Mr. *Treble,* my Cold is still so barbarous to refuse me that Pleasure! He, he, hem.

Treb. I'm very sorry for it, Madam: Methinks all Mankind should turn Physicians for the Cure on't.

Lady Fan. Why, truly, to give Mankind their due, there's few that know me but have offer'd their Remedy.

Treb. They have reason, Madam; for I know no body sings so near a Cherubim as your Ladyship.

Lady Fan. What I do, I owe chiefly to your Skill and Care, Mr. Treble. People do flatter me, indeed, that I have a Voice, and a *Je-ne-sçai-quoy* in the Conduct of it, that will make Musick of any thing. And truly I begin to believe so, since what happen'd t'other Night: Wou'd you think it, Mr. *Treble?* Walking pretty late in the Park, (for I often walk late in the Park, Mr *Treble*) a Whim took me to sing *Chevy Chase;* and, wou'd you believe it? next Morning I had three Copies of Verses, and six Billet-doux at my Levée upon it.

28

Treb. And without all dispute you deserv'd as many more, Madam. Are there any further Commands for your Ladyship's humble Servant?

Lady Fan. Nothing more at this Time, Mr. *Treble.* But I shall expect you here every Morning for this Month, to sing my little Matter there to me. I'll reward you for your Pains.

Treb. O Lord, Madam——

Lady Fan. Good-morrow, sweet Mr. *Treble.*

Treb. Your Ladyship's most obedient Servant.

[*Exit Treb.*

Enter Servant.

Serv. Will your Ladyship please to dine yet?

Lady Fan. Yes, let 'em serve. [*Exit Servant.*] Sure this *Heartfree* has bewitch'd me, *Madamoiselle.* You can't imagine how oddly he mixt himself in my Thoughts during my Rapture e'en now. I vow 'tis a thousand Pities he is not more polish'd: Don't you think so?

Madam. Matam, I tink it so great pity, dat if I was in your Ladyship place, I take him home in my House, I lock him up in my Closet, and I never let him go till I teach him every ting dat fine Laty expect from fine Gentelman.

Lady Fan. Why, truly, I believe I shou'd soon subdue his Brutality; for without doubt, he has a strange *Penchant* to grow fond of me, in spite of his Aversion to the Sex, else he wou'd ne'er have taken so much Pains about me. Lord, how proud wou'd some poor Creatures be of such a Conquest! But I, alas! I don't know how to receive as a Favour what I take to be so infinitely my Due. But what shall I do to new-mould him, *Madamoiselle?* for till then he's my utter Aversion.

Madam. Matam; you must laugh at him in all de place dat you meet him, and turn into de reticule all he say, and all he do.

Lady Fan. Why, truly, Satire has ever been of wondrous use to reform Ill-manners. Besides, 'tis my particular Talent to ridicule Folks. I can be severe, strangely severe, when I will, *Madamoiselle*——Give me the Pen and Ink——I find myself whimsical——I'll write to him——Or I'll let it alone, and be severe upon him that way [*Sitting down to write, rising up again.*]—Yet Active Severity is better than Passive. [*Sitting down.*]——'Tis as good let it alone, too; for every Lash I give him, perhaps, he'll take for a Favour. [*Rising.*]——Yet 'tis a thousand pities so much Satire should be lost. [*Sitting.*]—— But if it shou'd have a wrong Effect upon him, 'twould distract me. [*Rising.*]——Well, I must write, tho', after all, [*Sitting.*]——Or I'll let it alone, which is the same thing. [*Rising.*]

Madam. La voilà determinée.

[*Exeunt.*

ACT III.

Scene opens; Sir John, Lady Brute *and* Belinda *rising from the Table.*

Sir John. Here, take away the Things; I expect Company. But first bring me a Pipe; I'll smoak.

> [*To a Servant.*

Lady Brute. Lord, Sir *John,* I wonder you won't leave that nasty Custom.

Sir John. Pr'ythee, don't be impertinent.

Bel. [*To Lady Brute.*] I wonder who those People are he expects this Afternoon?

Lady Brute. I'd give the World to know: Perhaps 'tis *Constant*—he comes here sometimes: if it does prove him, I'm resolv'd I'll share the Visit.

Bel. We'll send for our Work, and sit here.

Lady Brute. He'll choak us with his Tobacco.

Bel. Nothing will choak us when we are doing what we have a mind to. *Lovewell!*

> Enter *Lovewell.*

Lov. Madam.

Lady Brute. Here; bring my Cousin's Work and mine hither.

> [*Exit Lov. and re-enters with their Work.*

Sir John. Whu! Pox, can't you work somewhere else?

Lady Brute. We shall be careful not to disturb you, Sir.

Bel. Your Pipe would make you too thoughtful, Uncle, if you were left alone; our Prittle-prattle will cure your Spleen.

Sir John. Will it so, Mrs. Pert? Now I believe it will so increase it, [*Sitting and smoaking.*] I shall take my own House for a Paper-mill.

Lady Brute. [*To Bel. aside.*] Don't let's mind him; let him say what he

31

will.

Sir John. A Woman's Tongue a Cure for the Spleen!—Oons—[*Aside.*] If a Man had got the Head-ach, they'd be for applying the same Remedy.

Lady Brute. You have done a great deal, *Belinda,* since yesterday.

Bel. Yes, I have work'd very hard; how do you like it?

Lady Brute. O, 'tis the prettiest Fringe in the World. Well, Cousin, you have the happiest Fancy: Pr'ythee, advise me about altering my Crimson Petticoat.

Sir John. A Pox o' your Petticoat! Here's such a Prating, a Man can't digest his own Thoughts for you.

Lady Brute. Don't answer him. [*Aside.*] Well, what do you advise me?

Bel. Why, really, I would not alter it at all. Methinks 'tis very pretty as it is.

Lady Brute. Ay, that's, true: But you know one grows weary of the prettiest things in the World, when one has had 'em long.

Sir John. Yes, I have taught her that.

Bel. Shall we provoke him a little?

Lady Brute. With all my Heart. *Belinda,* don't you long to be marry'd?

Bel. Why, there are some things in it I could like well enough.

Lady Brute. What do you think you shou'd dislike?

Bel. My Husband, a hundred to one else.

Lady Brute. O ye wicked Wretch! Sure you don't speak as you think?

Bel. Yes, I do: especially if he smoak'd Tobacco.

[*He looks earnestly at 'em.*

Lady Brute. Why, that many times takes off worse Smells.

Bel. Then he must smell very ill indeed.

Lady Brute. So some Men will, to keep their Wives from coming near 'em.

Bel. Then those Wives shou'd cuckold 'em at a distance.

He rises in a fury, throws his pipe at 'em, and drives 'em out. As they run off, Constant *and* Heartfree *enter.* Lady Brute *runs against* Constant.

Sir John. 'Oons, get you gone up Stairs, you confederating Strumpets you, o I'll cuckold you, with a Vengeance!

Lady Brute. O Lord, he'll beat us, he'll beat us. Dear, dear Mr. *Constant,* save us!

[*Exeunt.*

Sir John. I'll cuckold you, with a Pox.

Const. Heav'n! Sir *John,* what's the matter?

Sir John. Sure, if Women had been ready created, the Devil, instead of being kick'd down into Hell, had been marry'd.

Heart. Why, what new Plague have you found now?

Sir John. Why, these two Gentlewomen did but hear me say, I expected you here this Afternoon; upon which they presently resolv'd to take up the Room, o' purpose to plague me and my Friends.

Const. Was that all? Why, we shou'd have been glad of their Company.

Sir John. Then I should have been weary of yours; for I can't relish both together. They found fault with my smoaking Tobacco, too; and said Men stunk. But I have a good mind—to say something.

Const. No, nothing against the Ladies, pray.

Sir John. Split the Ladies! Come, will you sit down? Give us some Wine, Fellow: You won't smoak?

Const. No; nor drink, neither, at this time—I must ask your Pardon.

Sir John. What, this Mistress of yours runs in your Head! I'll warrant it's some such squeamish Minx as my Wife, that's grown so dainty of late, she finds fault even with a dirty Shirt.

Heart. That a Woman may do, and not be very dainty, neither.

Sir John. Pox o' the Women! let's drink. Come, you shall take one Glass, tho' I send for a Box of Lozenges to sweeten your Mouth after it.

33

Const. Nay, if one Glass will satisfy you, I'll drink it, without putting you to that Expence.

Sir John. Why, that's honest. Fill some Wine, Sirrah: So here's to you, Gentlemen—A Wife's the Devil. To your being both married.

[*They drink.*

Heart. O, your most humble Servant, Sir.

Sir John. Well, how do you like my Wine?

Const. 'Tis very good, indeed.

Heart. 'Tis admirable.

Sir John. Then give us t'other Glass.

Const. No, pray excuse us now: We'll come another time, and then we won't spare it.

Sir John. This one Glass, and no more: Come, it shall be your Mistress's Health: And that's a great Compliment from me, I assure you.

Const. And 'tis a very obliging one to me: So give us the Glasses.

Sir John. So: let her live—

[*Sir John coughs in the Glass.*

Heart. And be kind.

Const. What's the matter? Does it go the wrong way?

Sir John. If I had Love enough to be jealous, I shou'd take this for an ill Omen: For I never drank my Wife's Health in my Life, but I puk'd in the Glass.

Const. O, she's too virtuous to make a reasonable Man jealous.

Sir John. Pox of her Virtue! If I cou'd but catch her Adulterating, I might be divorc'd from her by Law.

Heart. And so pay her a yearly Pension, to be a distinguish'd Cuckold.

Enter Servant.

Serv. Sir, there's my Lord *Rake*, Colonel *Bully*, and some other Gentlemen at the *Blue-Posts*, desire your Company.

Sir John. Cod's so, we are to consult about playing the Devil to-night.

Heart. Well, we won't hinder Business.

Sir John. Methinks I don't know how to leave you, tho': But for once I must make bold. Or look you; may be the Conference mayn't last long: So, if you'll wait here half an hour, or an hour; if I don't come then— why, then—I won't come at all.

Heart. [*To Const.*] A good modest Proposition, truly!

[*Aside.*

Const. But let's accept on't, however. Who knows what may happen?

Heart. Well, Sir, to shew you how fond we are of your Company, we'll expect your Return as long as we can.

Sir John. Nay, may be I mayn't stay at all. But Business, you know, must be done. So your Servant—Or hark you, if you have a mind to take a Frisk with us, I have an Interest with my Lord; I can easily introduce you.

Const. We are much beholden to you; but for my part, I'm engag'd another way.

Sir John. What! to your Mistress, I'll warrant. Pr'ythee, leave your nasty Punk to entertain herself with her own lewd Thoughts, and make one with us to-night.

Const. Sir, 'tis Business that is to employ me.

Heart. And me; and Business must be done, you know.

Sir John. Ay, Women's Business, tho' the World were consum'd for't.

[*Exit Sir John.*

Const. Farewel, Beast! And now, my dear Friend, would my Mistress be but as complaisant as some Men's Wives, who think it a piece of good Breeding to receive the Visits of their Husband's Friends in his Absence!

Heart. Why, for your sake I could forgive her, tho' she should be so complaisant to receive something else in his Absence. But what way shall we invent to see her?

Const. O, ne'er hope it: Invention will prove as vain as Wishes.

Enter Lady Brute *and* Belinda.

Heart. What do you think now, Friend?

Const. I think I shall swoon.

Heart. I'll speak first, then, whilst you fetch breath.

Lady Brute. We think ourselves oblig'd, Gentlemen, to come and return you thanks for your Knight-Errantry. We were just upon being devour'd by the fiery Dragon.

Bel. Did not his Fumes almost knock you down, Gentlemen?

Heart. Truly, Ladies, we did undergo some Hardships; and should have done more, if some greater Heroes than ourselves, hard by, had not diverted him.

Const. Tho' I'm glad of the Service you are pleas'd to say we have done you, yet I'm sorry we could do it in no other way, than by making ourselves privy to what you would perhaps have kept a Secret.

Lady Brute. For Sir *John's* part, I suppose he design'd it no Secret, since he made so much Noise. And for myself, truly I'm not much concern'd, since 'tis fallen only into this Gentleman's Hands and yours; who, I have many Reasons to believe, will neither interpret nor report any thing to my disadvantage.

Const. Your good Opinion, Madam, was what I fear'd I never could have merited.

Lady Brute. Your Fears were vain, then, Sir; for I'm just to every body.

Heart. Pr'ythee, *Constant*, what is't you do to get the Ladies good Opinions? for I'm a Novice at it.

Bel. Sir, will you give me leave to instruct you?

Heart. Yes, that I will, with all my Soul, Madam.

Bel. Why, then, you must never be slovenly, never be out of humour, fare well and cry Roast-meat, smoak Tobacco, nor drink but when you are dry.

Heart. That's hard.

Const. Nay, if you take his Bottle from him, you break his Heart,

36

Madam.

Bel. Why, is it possible the Gentleman can love Drinking?

Heart. Only by way of Antidote.

Bel. Against what, pray?

Heart. Against Love, Madam.

Lady Brute. Are you afraid of being in Love, Sir?

Heart. I should, if there were any Danger of it.

Lady Brute. Pray why so?

Heart. Because I always had an Aversion to being us'd like a Dog.

Bel. Why, truly, Men in Love are seldom us'd better.

Lady Brute. But was you never in Love, Sir?

Heart. No, I thank Heav'n, Madam.

Bel. Pray, where got you your Learning, then?

Heart. From other People's Expence.

Bel. That's being a Spunger, Sir, which is scarce honest: If you'd buy some Experience with your own Money, as 'twould be fairlier got, so 'twould stick longer by you.

Enter Footman.

Foot. Madam, here's my Lady *Fancyfull*, to wait upon your Ladyship.

Lady Brute. Shield me, kind Heaven! What an Inundation of Impertinence is here coming upon us!

Enter Lady Fancyfull, *who runs first to* Lady Brute, *then to* Belinda, *kissing 'em.*

Lady Fan. My dear Lady *Brute*, and sweet *Belinda*, methinks 'tis an Age since I saw you.

Lady Brute. Yet 'tis but three Days; sure you have pass'd your time very ill, it seems so long to you.

Lady Fan. Why, really, to confess the truth to you, I am so everlastingly fatigu'd with the Addresses of unfortunate Gentlemen, that, were it not for the Extravagancy of the Example, I shou'd e'en tear out these wicked Eyes with my own Fingers, to make both myself and Mankind easy. What think you on't, Mr. *Heartfree*, for I take you to be my faithful Adviser?

Heart. Why, truly, Madam—I think—every Project that is for the good of Mankind ought to be encourag'd.

Lady Fan. Then I have your Consent, Sir?

Heart. To do whatever you please, Madam.

Lady Fan. You had a much more limited Complaisance this Morning, Sir. Would you believe it, Ladies? The Gentleman has been so exceeding generous, to tell me of above fifty Faults, in less time than it was well possible for me to commit two of 'em.

Const. Why, truly, Madam, my Friend there is apt to be something familiar with the Ladies.

Lady Fan. He is, indeed, Sir; but he's wondrous charitable with it: He has had the Goodness to design a Reformation, even down to my Fingers-ends.——'Twas thus, I think, Sir, [*Opening her fingers in an aukward manner.*] you'd have had 'em stand—My Eyes, too, he did not like: How was't you wou'd have directed 'em? Thus, I think. [*Staring at him.*]—Then there was something amiss in my Gait, too: I don't know well how 'twas; but as I take it, he would have had me walk like him. Pray, Sir, do me the Favour to take a turn or two about the Room, that the Company may see you.—He's sullen, Ladies, and won't. But, to make short, and give you as true an Idea as I can of the matter, I think 'twas much about this Figure, in general, he would have moulded me to: But I was an obstinate Woman, and could not resolve to make myself Mistress of his Heart, by growing as aukward as his Fancy.

[*She walks aukwardly about, staring and looking ungainly, then changes on a sudden to the Extremity of her usual Affectation.*

Heart. Just thus Women do, when they think we are in love with em, or when they are so with us.

[*Here Constant and Lady Brute talk together apart.*

Lady Fan. 'Twould, however, be less Vanity for me to conclude the former, than you the latter, Sir.

38

Heart. Madam, all I shall presume to conclude, is, That if I wer in love, you'd find the means to make me soon weary on't.

Lady Fan. Not by Over-fondness, upon my Word, Sir. But pray let's stop here; for you are so much govern'd by Instinct, I know you'll grow brutish at last.

Bel. [Aside.] Now am I sure she's fond of him: I'll try to make her jealous. Well, for my part, I should be glad to find somebody would be so free with me, that I might know my Faults, and mend 'em.

Lady Fan. Then pray let me recommend this Gentleman to you: I have known him some time, and will be Surety for him, that upon a very limited Encouragement on your side, you shall find an extended Impudence on his.

Heart. I thank you, Madam, for your Recommendation: But hating Idleness, I'm unwilling to enter into a Place where I believe there would be nothing to do. I was fond of serving your Ladyship, because I knew you'd find me constant Employment.

Lady Fan. I told you he'd be rude, *Belinda.*

Bel. O, a little Bluntness is a sign of Honesty, which makes me always ready to pardon it. So, Sir, if you have no other Exceptions to my Service, but the fear of being idle in it, you may venture to lift yourself: I shall find you Work, I warrant you.

Heart. Upon those Terms I engage, Madam; and this (with your leave) I take for Earnest.

[*Offering to kiss her Hand.*

Bel. Hold there, Sir; I'm none of your Earnest-givers. But if I'm well serv'd, I give good Wages, and pay punctually.

[*Heartf. and Bel. seem to continue talking familiarly.*

Lady Fan. [Aside.] I don't like this jesting between 'em——Methinks the Fool begins to look as if he were in earnest.——But then he must be a Fool, indeed.——Lard, what a Difference there is between me and her! [*Looking at Bel. scornfully.*] How I shou'd despise such a Thing, if I were a Man!——What a Nose she has!—What a Chin——What a Neck!—— Then her Eyes——And the worst kissing Lips in the Universe——No, no, he can never like her, that's positive——Yet I can't suffer 'em together any longer. Mr. *Heartfree,* do you know that you and I must

39

have no Quarrel for all this? I can't forbear being a little severe now and then: But Women, you know, may be allowed any thing.

Heart. Up to a certain Age, Madam.

Lady Fan. Which I'm not yet past, I hope.

Heart. [*Aside.*] Nor never will, I dare swear.

Lady Fan. [*To Lady Brute.*] Come, Madam, will your Ladyship be Witness to our Reconciliation?

Lady Brute. You agree, then, at last?

Heart. [*Slightingly.*] We forgive.

Lady Fan. [*Aside.*] That was a cold, ill-natur'd Reply.

Lady Brute. Then there's no Challenges sent between you?

Heart. Not from me, I promise. [*Aside to Constant.*] But that's more than I'll do for her; for I know she can as well be damn'd as forbear writing to me.

Const. That I believe. But I think we had best be going, lest she should suspect something, and be malicious.

Heart. With all my heart.

Const. Ladies, we are your humble Servants. I see Sir *John* is quite engag'd, 'twould be in vain to expect him. Come, *Heartfree*.

[*Exit.*

Heart. Ladies, your Servant. [*To Belinda.*] I hope, Madam, you won't forget our Bargain; I'm to say what I please to you.

[*Exit Heartfree.*

Bel. Liberty of Speech entire, Sir.

Lady Fan. [*Aside.*] Very pretty truly—But how the Blockhead went out —languishing at her, and not a Look toward me!—Well, Churchmen may talk, but Miracles are not ceas'd. For 'tis more than natural, such a rude Fellow as he, and such a little Impertinent as she, should be capable of making a Woman of my Sphere uneasy. But I can bear her sight no longer——methinks she's grown ten times uglier than *Cornet*. I must home, and study Revenge. [*To Lady Brute.*] Madam, your humble Servant; I must take my leave.

Lady Brute. What, going already, Madam?

Lady Fan. I must beg you'll excuse me this once; for really I have eighteen Visits to return this Afternoon: So you see I'm importun'd by the Women as well as the Men.

Bel. [*Aside.*] And she's quits with them both.

Lady Fan. [*Going.*] Nay, you shan't go one Step out of the Room.

Lady Brute. Indeed I'll wait upon you down.

Lady Fan. No, sweet Lady *Brute*, you know I swoon at Ceremony.

Lady Brute. Pray give me leave.

Lady Fan. You know I won't.

Lady Brute. Indeed I must.

Lady Fan. Indeed you shan't.

Lady Brute. Indeed I will.

Lady Fan. Indeed you shan't.

Lady Brute. Indeed I will.

Lady Fan. Indeed you shan't. Indeed, indeed, indeed you shan't.

[*Exit Lady Fan. running; they follow.*

Re-enter Lady Brute, *sola.*

This impertinent Woman has put me out of Humour for a Fortnight ——What an agreeable Moment has her foolish Visit interrupted! Lord, how like a Torrent Love flows into the Heart, when once the Sluice of Desire is open'd! Good Gods! What a Pleasure there is in doing what we should not do!

Re-enter Constant.

Ha! here again?

Const. Tho' the renewing my Visit may seem a little irregular, I hope I shall obtain your Pardon for it, Madam, when you know I only left the Room, lest the Lady who was here should have been as malicious in her

Remarks as she's foolish in her Conduct.

Lady Brute. He who has Discretion enough to be tender of a Woman's Reputation, carries a Virtue about him may atone for a great many Faults.

Const. If it has a Title to atone for any, its Pretensions must needs be strongest where the Crime is Love. I therefore hope I shall be forgiven the Attempt I have made upon your Heart, since my Enterprize has been a Secret to all the World but yourself.

Lady Brute. Secrecy, indeed, in Sins of this kind, is an Argument of weight to lessen the Punishment; but nothing's a Plea for a Pardon entire, without a sincere Repentance.

Const. If Sincerity in Repentance consists in Sorrow for offending, no Cloyster ever inclos'd so true a Penitent as I should be. But I hope it cannot be reckon'd an Offence to love where 'tis a Duty to adore.

Lady Brute. 'Tis an Offence, a great one, where it would rob a Woman of all she ought to be ador'd for—her Virtue.

Const. Virtue?—Virtue, alas! is no more like the thing that's call'd so, than 'tis like Vice itself. Virtue consists in Goodness, Honour, Gratitude, Sincerity, and Pity; and not in peevish, snarling, strait-lac'd Chastity. True Virtue, wheresoever it moves, still carries an intrinsick Worth about it, and is in every Place, and in each Sex, of equal Value. So is not Continence, you see: That Phantom of Honour, which Men in every Age have so contemned, they have thrown it amongst the Women to scrabble for.

Lady Brute. If it be a thing of so little Value, why do you so earnestly recommend it to your Wives and Daughters?

Const. We recommend it to our Wives, Madam, because we wou'd keep 'em to ourselves; and to our Daughters, because we wou'd dispose of 'em to others.

Lady Brute. 'Tis then, of some Importance, it seems, since you can't dispose of them without it.

Const. That Importance, Madam, lies in the Humour of the Country, not in the Nature of the Thing.

Lady Brute. How do you prove that, Sir?

Const. From the Wisdom of a neighbouring Nation in a contrary Practice. In Monarchies, things go by Whimsy; but Commonwealths weigh all things in the Scale of Reason.

Lady Brute. I hope we are not so very light a People, to bring up Fashions without some ground.

Const. Pray what does your Ladyship think of a powder'd Coat for deep Mourning?

Lady Brute. I think, Sir, your Sophistry has all the effect that you can reasonably expect it should have; it puzzles, but don't convince.

Const. I'm sorry for it.

Lady Brute. I'm sorry to hear you say so.

Const. Pray why?

Lady Brute. Because, if you expected more from it, you have a worse Opinion of my Understanding than I desire you should have.

Const. [*Aside.*] I comprehend her: She would have me set a Value upon her Chastity, that I might think myself the more oblig'd to her when she makes me a Present of it. [*To her.*] I beg you will believe I did but rally, Madam; I know you judge too well of Right and Wrong, to be deceiv'd by Arguments like those. I hope you'll have so favourable an Opinion of my Understanding too, to believe the thing call'd Virtue has Worth enough with me, to pass for an eternal Obligation where'er 'tis sacrific'd.

Lady Brute. It is, I think, so great a one as nothing can repay.

Const. Yes; the making the Man you love your everlasting Debtor.

Lady Brute. When Debtors once have borrow'd all we have to lend, they are very apt to grow shy of their Creditors' Company.

Const. That, Madam, is only when they are forc'd to borrow of Usurers, and not of a generous Friend. Let us choose our Creditors, and we are seldom so ungrateful to shun 'em.

Lady Brute. What think you of Sir *John*, Sir? I was his free Choice.

Const. I think he's married, Madam.

Lady Brute. Does Marriage, then, exclude Men from your Rule of

43

Constancy?

Const. It does. Constancy's a brave, free, haughty, generous Agent, that cannot buckle to the Chains of Wedlock. There's a poor sordid Slavery in Marriage, that turns the flowing Tide of Honour, and sinks us to the lowest Ebb of Infamy. 'Tis a corrupted Soil: Ill-Nature, Avarice, Sloth, Cowardice, and Dirt, are all its Product.

Lady Brute. Have you no Exceptions to this general Rule, as well as to t'other?

Const. Yes; I would, after all, be an Exception to it myself, if you were free in Power and Will to make me so.

Lady Brute. Compliments are well plac'd where 'tis impossible to lay hold on 'em.

Const. I wou'd to Heaven 'twere possible for you to lay hold on mine, that you might see it is no Compliment at all. But since you are already dispos'd of, beyond Redemption, to one who does not know the Value of the Jewel you have put into his Hands, I hope you wou'd not think him greatly wrong'd, tho' it should sometimes be look'd on by a Friend, who knows how to esteem it as he ought.

Lady Brute. If looking on't alone wou'd serve his turn, the Wrong, perhaps, might not be very great.

Const. Why, what if he shou'd wear it now and then a Day, so he gave good Security to bring it home again at Night?

Lady Brute. Small Security, I fancy, might serve for that. One might venture to take his Word.

Const. Then, where's the Injury to the Owner?

Lady Brute. 'Tis an Injury to him, if he think it one. For if Happiness be seated in the Mind, Unhappiness must be so too.

Const. Here I close with you, Madam, and draw my conclusive Argument from your own Position: If the Injury lie in the Fancy, there needs nothing but Secrecy to prevent the Wrong.

Lady Brute. [*Going.*] A surer way to prevent it, is to hear no more Arguments in its behalf.

Const. [*Following her.*] But, Madam——

Lady Brute. But, Sir, 'tis my turn to be discreet now, and not suffer too long a Visit.

Const. [*Catching her Hand.*] By Heaven, you shall not stir, till you give me hopes that I shall see you again at some more convenient Time and Place!

Lady Brute. I give you just hopes enough——[*Breaking from him.*] to get loose from you: and that's all I can afford you at this time.

[*Exit running.*

Constant *solus.*

Now, by all that's great and good, she is a charming Woman! In what Extasy of Joy she has left me! For she gave me Hope, did she not say she gave me Hope?—Hope! Ay: what Hope? Enough to make me let her go —Why, that's enough in Conscience. Or, no matter how 'twas spoke: Hope was the Word: it came from her, and it was said to me.

Enter Heartfree.

Ha, *Heartfree!* Thou hast done me noble Service in prattling to the young Gentlewoman without there; come to my Arms, thou venerable Bawd, and let me squeeze thee [*Embracing him eagerly.*] as a new Pair of Stays does a fat Country Girl, when she's carried to Court to stand for a Maid of Honour.

Heart. Why, what the Devil's all this Rapture for?

Const. Rapture! There's ground for Rapture, Man; there's Hopes, my *Heartfree,* Hopes, my Friend!

Heart. Hopes! of what?

Const. Why, Hopes that my Lady and I together (for 'tis more than one Body's Work) should make Sir *John* a Cuckold.

Heart. Pr'ythee, what did she say to thee?

Const. Say? What did she not say? She said that——says she—she said —Zoons, I don't know what she said; but she look'd as if she said every thing I'd have her. And so, if thou'lt go to the Tavern, I'll treat thee with any thing that Gold can buy; I'll give all my Silver amongst the Drawers, make a Bonfire before the Door; say the Plenipo's have sign'd the Peace, and the Bank of *England's* grown honest.

45

Scene opens; Lord Rake, Sir John, *&c. at a Table, drinking.*

All. Huzza!

Lord Rake. Come, Boys, charge again——So—Confusion to all Order! Here's Liberty of Conscience.

All. Huzza!

Lord Rake. I'll sing you a Song I made this Morning to this purpose.

Sir John. 'Tis wicked, I hope.

Col. Bully. Don't my Lord tell you he made it?

Sir John. Well, then, let's ha't.

Lord *Rake* Sings.

I.

What a pother of late
Have they kept in the State,
About setting our Consciences free!
A Bottle has more
Dispensations in store,
Than the King and the State can decree.

II.

When my Head's full of Wine,
I o'erflow with Design,
And know no Penal-Laws that can curb me:
Whate'er I devise
Seems good in my Eyes,
And Religion ne'er dares to disturb me.

III.

No saucy remorse
Intrudes in my course,
Nor impertinent notions of evil;
So there's claret in store,
In peace I've my whore,
And in peace I jog on to the devil.

All sing. So there's Claret, &c.

Lord Rake. [*Rep.*] *And in Peace I jog on to the Devil.* Well, how do you like it, Gentlemen?

All. O, admirable!

Sir John. I would not give a Fig for a Song that is not full of Sin and Impudence.

Lord Rake. Then my Muse is to your Taste. But drink away; the Night steals upon us; we shall want Time to be lewd in. Hey, Page! Sally out, Sirrah, and see what's doing in the Camp; we'll beat up their Quarters presently.

Page. I'll bring your Lordship an exact Account.

[*Exit Page.*

Lord Rake. Now let the Spirit of Clary go round. Fill me a Brimmer Here's to our Forlorn Hope. Courage, Knight, Victory attends you.

Sir John. And Laurels shall crown me; drink away, and be damn'd.

Lord Rake. Again, Boys; t'other Glass, and damn Morality.

Sir John. [*Drunk.*] Ay—damn Morality—and damn the Watch. And let the Constable be married.

All. Huzza!

Re-enter Page.

Lord Rake. How are the Streets inhabited, Sirrah?

Page. My Lord, 'tis Sunday-night; they are full of drunken Citizens.

Lord Rake. Along, then, Boys, we shall have a Feast.

Col. Bully. Along, noble Knight.

Sir John. Ay——along, *Bully*; and he that says Sir *John Brute* is not as drunk and as religious as the drunkenest Citizen of them all—is a Liar, and the Son of a Whore.

Col. Bully. Why, that was bravely spoke, and like a free-born *Englishman.*

Sir John. What's that to you, Sir, whether I am an *Englishman* or a *Frenchman?*

Col. Bully. Zoons, you are not angry, Sir?

Sir John. Zoons, I am angry, Sir——for if I'm a free-born *Englishman,* what have you to do even to talk of my Privileges?

Lord Rake. Why, pr'ythee, Knight, don't quarrel here; leave private Animosities to be decided by Day-light; let the Night be employ'd against the publick Enemy.

Sir John. My Lord, I respect you because you are a Man of Quality. But I'll make that Fellow know, I am within a Hair's breadth as absolute by my Privileges, as the King of *France* is by his Prerogative. He by his Prerogative takes Money where it is not his due; I by my Privilege refuse paying it where I owe it. Liberty and Property, and *Old England,* Huzza!

All. Huzza!

[*Exit Sir John reeling, all following him.*

Scene, *A Bed-Chamber.*

Enter Lady Brute *and* Belinda.

Lady Brute. Sure 'tis late, *Belinda*; I begin to be sleepy.

Bel. Yes, 'tis near Twelve. Will you go to Bed?

Lady Brute. To Bed, my Dear? And by that time I am fallen into a sweet Sleep (or perhaps a sweet Dream, which is better and better) Sir *John* will come home roaring drunk, and be overjoy'd he finds me in a Condition to be disturb'd.

Bel. O, you need not fear him; he's in for all Night. The Servants say he's gone to drink with my Lord *Rake.*

Lady Brute. Nay, 'tis not very likely, indeed, such suitable Company should part presently. What Hogs Men turn, *Belinda,* when they grow weary of Women!

Bel. And what Owls they are, whilst they are fond of 'em!

Lady Brute. But That we may forgive well enough, because they are so upon our accounts.

48

Bel. We ought to do so, indeed; but 'tis a hard matter. For when a Man is really in love, he looks so unsufferably silly, that tho' a Woman lik'd him well enough before, she has then much ado to endure the Sight of him: And this I take to be the Reason why Lovers are so generally ill-us'd.

Lady Brute. Well, I own, now, I'm well enough pleased to see a Man look like an Ass for me.

Bel. Ay, I'm pleas'd he should look like an Ass, too;—that is, I'm pleased with myself for making him look so.

Lady Brute. Nay, truly, I think if he'd find some other way to express his Passion, 'twould be more to his advantage.

Bel. Yes; for then a Woman might like his Passion and him too.

Lady Brute. Yet, *Belinda,* after all, a Woman's Life would be but a dull Business, if it were not for Men; and Men that can look like Asses, too. We shou'd never blame Fate for the shortness of our Days; our Time would hang wretchedly upon our Hands.

Bel. Why, truly, they do help us off with a good share on't: For were there no Men in the World, o'my Conscience, I shou'd be no longer a-dressing than I'm a-saying my Prayers; nay, tho' it were Sunday: For you know that one may go to Church without Stays on.

Lady Brute. But don't you think Emulation might do something? For every Woman you see desires to be finer than her Neighbour.

Bel. That's only that the Men may like her better than her Neighbour. No, if there were no Men, adieu fine Petticoats, we should be weary of wearing 'em.

Lady Brute. And adieu Plays, we should be weary of seeing 'em.

Bel. Adieu *Hyde Park,* the Dust would choak us.

Lady Brute. Adieu *St. James's,* walking would tire us.

Bel. Adieu *London,* the Smoke would stifle us.

Lady Brute. And adieu going to Church, for Religion wou'd ne'er prevail with us.

Both. Ha! ha! ha! ha! ha!

49

Bel. Our Confession is so very hearty, sure we merit Absolution.

Lady Brute. Not unless we go thro' with't, and confess all. So, pr'ythee, for the Ease of our Consciences, let's hide nothing.

Bel. Agreed.

Lady Brute. Why, then, I confess, that I love to sit in the Fore-front of a Box; for if one sits behind, there's two Acts gone, perhaps, before one's found out. And when I am there, if I perceive the Men whispering and looking upon me, you must know I cannot for my Life forbear thinking they talk to my Advantage; and that sets a thousand little tickling Vanities on foot——

Bel. Just my Case, for all the World; but go on.

Lady Brute. I watch with Impatience for the next Jest in the Play, that I might laugh, and shew my white Teeth. If the Poet has been dull, and the Jest be long *a-coming*, I pretend to whisper one to my Friend, and from thence fall into a little small Discourse, in which I take occasion to shew my Face in all Humours, brisk, pleas'd, serious, melancholy, languishing——Not that what we say to one another causes any of these alterations. But——

Bel. Don't trouble yourself to explain. For if I'm not mistaken, you and I have had some of these necessary Dialogues before now with the same Intention.

Lady Brute. Why, I swear, *Belinda*, some People do give strange agreeable Airs to their Faces in speaking. Tell me true—Did you never practise in the Glass?

Bel. Why, did you?

Lady Brute. Yes, 'faith, many a time.

Bel. And I too, I own it; both how to speak myself, and how to look when others speak. But my Glass and I could never yet agree what Face I should make when they come blunt out with a nasty thing in a Play: For all the Men presently look upon the Women, that's certain: so laugh we must not, tho' our Stays burst for't, because that's telling Truth, and owning we understand the Jest. And to look serious is so dull, when the whole House is a laughing—

Lady Brute. Besides, that looking serious does really betray our Knowledge in the matter, as much as laughing with the Company would do: For if we did not understand the thing, we shou'd naturally do like other People.

Bel. For my part, I always take that occasion to blow my Nose.

Lady Brute. You must blow your Nose half off, then, at some Plays.

Bel. Why don't some Reformer or other be at the Poet for't?

Lady Brute. Because he is not so sure of our private Approbation, as of our publick Thanks. Well, sure there is not upon Earth so impertinent a thing as Women's Modesty.

Bel. Yes: Men's Fantasque, that obliges us to it. If we quit our Modesty, they say we lose our Charms: and yet they know that very Modesty is Affectation, and rail at our Hypocrisy.

Lady Brute. Thus, one would think 'twere a hard matter to please 'em, Niece; yet our kind Mother Nature has given us something that makes amends for all. Let our Weakness be what it will, Mankind will still be weaker; and whilst there is a World, 'tis Woman that will govern it. But, pr'ythee, one Word of poor *Constant* before we go to bed, if it be but to furnish matter for Dreams: I dare swear he's talking of me now, or thinking of me at least, tho' it be in the middle of his Prayers.

Bel. So he ought, I think; for you were pleas'd to make him a good round Advance to-day, Madam.

Lady Brute. Why, I have e'en plagu'd him enough to satisfy any reasonable Woman: He has besieg'd me these two Years, to no purpose.

Bel. And if he besieg'd you two Years more, he'd be well enough pay'd, so he had the plundering of you at last.

Lady Brute. That may be; but I'm afraid the Town won't be able to hold out much longer: for to confess the Truth to you, *Belinda*, the Garrison begins to grow mutinous.

Bel. Then the sooner you capitulate, the better.

Lady Brute. Yet, methinks, I wou'd fain stay a little longer to see you fix'd too, that we might start together, and see who cou'd love longest. What think you, if *Heartfree* shou'd have a Month's Mind to you?

Bel. Why, 'faith, I cou'd almost be in love with him for despising that foolish, affected Lady *Fancyfull*; but I'm afraid he's too cold ever to warm himself by my Fire.

Lady Brute. Then he deserves to be froze to death. Wou'd I were a Man for your sake, dear Rogue! [*Kissing her.*]

Bel. You'd wish yourself a Woman again for your own, or the Men are mistaken. But if I cou'd make a Conquest of this Son of *Bacchus*, and rival his Bottle, what shou'd I do with him? He has no Fortune, I can't marry him: and sure you wou'd not have me commit Fornication?

Lady Brute. Why, if you did, Child, 'twould be but a good friendly part; if 'twere only to keep me in countenance whilst I commit—you know what.

Bel. Well, if I can't resolve to serve you that way, I may perhaps some other, as much to your Satisfaction. But pray how shall we contrive to see these Blades again quickly?

Lady Brute. We must e'en have recourse to the old way; make 'em an Appointment 'twixt Jest and Earnest; 'twill look like a Frolick, and that you know 's a very good thing to save a Woman's Blushes.

Bel. You advise well; but where shall it be?

Lady Brute. In *Spring Garden.* But they shan't know their Women, till their Women pull off their Masks; for a Surprize is the most agreeable thing in the World: And I find myself in a very good Humour, ready to do 'em any good turn I can think on.

Bel. Then pray write 'em the necessary Billet, without farther delay.

Lady Brute. Let's go into your Chamber, then, and whilst you say your Prayers I'll do it, Child.

[*Exeunt.*

ACT IV.

Scene, Covent Garden.

Enter Lord Rake, Sir John, *&c. with swords drawn.*

Lord Rake. Is the Dog dead?

Col. Bully. No, damn him, I heard him wheeze.

Lord Rake. How the Witch his Wife howl'd!

Col. Bully. Ay, she'll alarm the Watch presently.

Lord Rake. Appear, Knight, then; come, you have a good Cause to fight for—there's a Man murder'd.

Sir John. Is there? Then let his Ghost be satisfy'd; for I'll sacrifice a Constable to it presently, and burn his Body upon his wooden Chair.

Enter a Taylor, *with a bundle under his arm.*

Col. Bully. How now? What have we got here? A Thief.

Taylor. No, an't please you, I'm no Thief.

Lord Rake. That we'll see presently: Here, let the General examine him.

Sir John. Ay, ay, let me examine him, and I'll lay a hundred Pound I find him guilty, in spite of his Teeth—for he looks—like a—sneaking Rascal. Come, Sirrah, without Equivocation or mental Reservation, tell me of what Opinion you are, and what Calling; for by them——I shall guess at your Morals.

Taylor. An't please you, I'm a Dissenting Journeyman Taylor.

Sir John. Then, Sirrah, you love Lying by your Religion, and Theft by your Trade: And so, that your Punishment may be suitable to your Crimes—I'll have you first gagg'd—and then hang'd.

Tayl. Pray, good worthy Gentlemen, don't abuse me: indeed I'm an honest Man, and a good Workman, tho' I say it, that should not say it.

Sir John. No Words, Sirrah, but attend your Fate.

Lord Rake. Let me see what's in that Bundle.

Tayl. An't please you, it is the Doctor of the Parish's Gown.

Lord Rake. The Doctor's Gown!——Hark you, Knight, you won't stick at abusing the Clergy, will you?

Sir John. No, I'm drunk, and I'll abuse any thing—but my Wife; and her I name—with Reverence.

Lord Rake. Then you shall wear this Gown, whilst you charge the Watch; that tho' the Blows fall upon you, the Scandal may light upon the Church.

Sir John. A generous Design——by all the Gods——give it me.

> [*Takes the Gown, and puts it on.*

Tayl. O dear Gentlemen, I shall be quite undone, if you take the Gown.

Sir John. Retire, Sirrah; and since you carry off your Skin—go home and be happy.

Tayl. [*Pausing.*] I think I had e'en as good follow the Gentleman's friendly Advice; for if I dispute any longer, who knows but the Whim may take him to case me? These Courtiers are fuller of Tricks than they are of Money; they'll sooner cut a Man's Throat, than pay his Bill.

> [*Exit Taylor.*

Sir John. So, how do you like my Shapes now?

Lord Rake. This will do to a Miracle; he looks like a Bishop going to the Holy War. But to your Arms, Gentlemen, the Enemy appears.

Enter Constable *and* Watch.

Watch. Stand! Who goes there? Come before the Constable.

Sir John. The Constable is a Rascal——and you are the Son of a Whore.

Watch. A good civil Answer for a Parson, truly!

Constab. Methinks, Sir, a Man of your Coat might set a better Example.

Sir John. Sirrah, I'll make you know——there are Men of my Coat can set as bad Examples——as you can do, you Dog, you.

> [*Sir John strikes the Constable. They knock him down, disarm him, and*

Constab. So, we have secur'd the Parson, however.

Sir John. Blood, and Blood——and Blood.

Watch. Lord have mercy upon us! How the wicked Wretch raves of Blood! I'll warrant he has been murdering some body to-night.

Sir John. Sirrah, there's nothing got by Murder but a Halter: My Talent lies towards Drunkenness and Simony.

Watch. Why, that now was spoke like a Man of Parts, Neighbours; 'tis pity he shou'd be so disguised.

Sir John. You lye——I'm not disguis'd; for I am drunk barefac'd.

Watch. Look you there again—This is a mad Parson, Mr. *Constable;* I'll lay a Pot of Ale upon 's Head, he's a good Preacher.

Constab. Come, Sir, out of respect to your Calling, I shan't put you into the Round-house; but we must secure you in our Drawing-room till Morning, that you may do no Mischief. So, come along.

Sir John. You may put me where you will, Sirrah, now you have overcome me——But if I can't do Mischief, I'll think of Mischief—in spite of your Teeth, you Dog, you.

[*Exeunt.*

Scene, *A Bed-Chamber.*

Enter Heartfree, *solus.*

What the Plague ails me?——Love? No, I thank you for that, my Heart's Rock still——Yet 'tis *Belinda* that disturbs me; that's positive ——Well, what of all that? Must I love her for being troublesome? At that rate I might love all the Women I meet, I'gad. But hold!—Tho' I don't love her for disturbing me, yet she may disturb me, because I love her——Ay, that may be, 'faith. I have dreamt of her, that's certain—— Well, so I have of my Mother; therefore what's that to the purpose? Ay, but *Belinda* runs in my Mind waking—and so does many a damn'd thing that I don't care a Farthing for——Methinks, tho', I would fain be talking to her, and yet I have no Business——Well, am I the first Man that has had a Mind to do an impertinent thing?

Enter Constant.

55

Const. How now, *Heartfree?* What makes you up and dress'd so soon? I thought none but Lovers quarrell'd with their Beds; I expected to have found you snoring, as I us'd to do.

Heart. Why, 'faith, Friend, 'tis the Care I have of your Affairs, that makes me so thoughtful; I have been studying all Night how to bring your matter about with *Belinda.*

Const. With *Belinda?*

Heart. With my Lady, I mean: And, 'faith, I have mighty Hopes on't. Sure you must be very well satisfied with her Behaviour to you yesterday?

Const. So well, that nothing but a Lover's Fears can make me doubt of Success. But what can this sudden Change proceed from?

Heart. Why, you saw her Husband beat her, did you not?

Const. That's true: A Husband is scarce to be borne upon any terms, much less when he fights with his Wife. Methinks, she shou'd e'en have cuckolded him upon the very spot, to shew that after the Battle she was Master of the Field.

Heart. A Council of War of Women wou'd infallibly have advis'd her to't. But, I confess, so agreeable a Woman as *Belinda* deserves better Usage.

Const. Belinda again!

Heart. My Lady, I mean. What a Pox makes me blunder so to-day? [*Aside.*] A Plague of this treacherous Tongue!

Const. Pr'ythee, look upon me seriously, *Heartfree*—Now answer me directly: Is it my Lady, or *Belinda*, employs your careful Thoughts thus?

Heart. My Lady, or *Belinda?*

Const. In Love; by this Light, in Love.

Heart. In Love!

Const. Nay, ne'er deny it; for thou'lt do it so aukwardly, 'twill but make the Jest sit heavier about thee. My dear Friend, I give thee much Joy.

Heart. Why, pr'ythee, you won't persuade me to it, will you?

56

Const. That she's Mistress of your Tongue, that's plain; and I know you are so honest a Fellow, your Tongue and Heart always go together. But how, but how the Devil? Pha, ha, ha, ha—

Heart. Hey-dey! Why, sure you don't believe it in earnest?

Const. Yes, I do, because I see you deny it in jest.

Heart. Nay, but look you, *Ned*—a——deny in jest——a——gadzooks, you know I say——a——when a Man denies a thing in jest—a—

Const. Pha, ha, ha, ha, ha.

Heart. Nay, then we shall have it: What, because a Man stumbles at a Word: did you never make a Blunder?

Const. Yes; for I am in Love, I own it.

Heart. Then, so am I—Now laugh till thy Soul's glutted with Mirth. [*Embracing him.*] But, dear *Constant*, don't tell the Town on't.

Const. Nay, then, 'twere almost pity to laugh at thee, after so honest a Confession. But tell us a little, *Jack*, by what new-invented Arms has this mighty Stroke been given?

Heart. E'en by that unaccountable Weapon call'd *Je-ne-sçai-quoy*: For every thing that can come within the Verge of Beauty, I have seen it with indifference.

Const. So in few Words, then, the *Je-ne-sçai-quoy* has been too hard for the quilted Petticoat.

Heart. I'gad, I think the *Je-ne-sçai-quoy* is in the quilted Petticoat; at least 'tis certain, I ne'er think on't without——a——a *Je-ne-sçai-quoy* in every Part about me.

Const. Well, but have all your Remedies lost their Virtue? Have you turn'd her inside out yet?

Heart. I dare not so much as think on't.

Const. But don't the two Years Fatigue I have had discourage you?

Heart. Yes: I dread what I foresee; yet cannot quit the Enterprize. Like some Soldiers, whose Courage dwells more in their Honour, than their Nature—on they go, tho' the Body trembles at what the Soul makes it undertake.

Const. Nay, if you expect your Mistress will use you as your Profanations against her Sex deserve, you tremble justly. But how do you intend to proceed, Friend?

Heart. Thou know'st I'm but a Novice; be friendly, and advise me.

Const. Why, look you, then: I'd have you—Serenade and a——write a Song——Go to Church; Look like a Fool——Be very officious; Ogle, write and lead out: And who knows but in a Year or two's time you may *be*——call'd a troublesome Puppy, and sent about your Business.

Heart. That's hard.

Const. Yet thus it oft falls out with Lovers, Sir.

Heart. Pox on me for making one of the Number!

Const. Have a care: Say no saucy things; 'twill but augment your Crime; and if your Mistress hears on't, increase your Punishment.

Heart. Pr'ythee say something, then, to encourage me; you know I help'd you in your Distress.

Const. Why, then, to encourage you to Perseverance, tho' you may be thoroughly ill-us'd for your Offences; I'll put you in mind, that even the coyest Ladies of 'em all are made up of Desires, as well as we; and tho' they do hold out a long time, they will capitulate at last. For that thundering Engineer, Nature, does make such havock in the Town, they must surrender at long run, or perish in their own Flames.

Enter a Footman.

Foot. Sir, there's a Porter without with a Letter; he desires to give it into your own Hands.

Const. Call him in.

Enter Porter.

Const. What, *Joe!* Is it thee?

Porter. An't please you, Sir, I was order'd to deliver this into your own Hands by two well-shap'd Ladies, at the *New Exchange*. I was at your Honour's Lodgings, and your Servants sent me hither.

Const. 'Tis well; are you to carry any Answer?

Porter. No, my noble Master. They gave me my Orders, and whip they were gone, like a Maidenhead at Fifteen.

Const. Very well; there.

[*Gives him Money.*

Porter. God bless your Honour!

[*Exit Porter.*

Const. Now let's see what honest, trusty *Joe* has brought us.

Reads.

If you and your play-fellow can spare time from your business and devotions, don't fail to be at *Spring-Garden* about eight in the evening. You'll find nothing there but women, so you need bring no other arms than what you usually carry about you.

So, Play-fellow: here's something to stay your Stomach till your Mistress's Dish is ready for you.

Heart. Some of our old batter'd Acquaintance. I won't go, not I.

Const. Nay, that you can't avoid; there's Honour in the Case; 'tis a Challenge, and I want a Second.

Heart. I doubt I shall be but a very useless one to you; for I'm so dishearten'd by this Wound *Belinda* has given me, I don't think I shall have Courage enough to draw my Sword.

Const. O, if that be all, come along; I'll warrant you find Sword enough for such Enemies as we have to deal withal.

[*Exeunt.*

Scene, *A Street.*

Enter Constable, *&c. with* Sir John.

Constab. Come along, Sir; I thought to have let you slip this Morning, because you were a Minister; but you are as drunk and as abusive as ever. We'll see what the Justice of the Peace will say to you.

Sir John. And you shall see what I'll say to the Justice of the Peace, Sirrah.

Enter Servant.

Constab. Pray, acquaint his Worship, we have got an unruly Parson here: We are unwilling to expose him, but don't know what to do with him.

Serv. I'll acquaint my Master.

[Exit Serv.

Sir John. You——Constable—What damn'd Justice is this?

Constab. One that will take Care of you, I warrant you.

Enter Justice.

Just. Well, Mr. Constable, what's the Disorder here?

Constab. An't please your Worship——

Sir John. Let me speak, and be damn'd: I'm a Divine, and can unfold Mysteries better than you can do.

Just. Sadness, sadness! A Minister so overtaken! Pray, Sir, give the Constable leave to speak, and I'll hear you very patiently: I assure you, Sir, I will.

Sir John. Sir——You are a very civil Magistrate! Your most humble Servant.

Constab. An't please your Worship, then, he has attempted to beat the Watch to-night, and swore——

Sir John. You lye.

Just. Hold, pray, Sir, a little.

Sir John. Sir, your very humble Servant.

Constab. Indeed, Sir, he came at us without any Provocation, call'd us Whores and Rogues, and laid us on with a great Quarter-staff. He was in my Lord *Rake's Company*: They have been playing the Devil to-night.

Just. Hem——Hem——Pray, Sir——may you be Chaplain to my Lord?

60

Sir John. Sir——I presume——I may if I will.

Just. My meaning, Sir, is——Are you so?

Sir John. Sir—You mean very well.

Just. He, hem——hem——Under Favour, Sir, pray answer me directly.

Sir John. Under Favour, Sir——Do you use to answer directly when you are drunk?

Just. Good lack, good lack! Here's nothing to be got from him: Pray, Sir, may I crave your Name?

Sir John. Sir——My Name's——[*He hiccups.*] Hiccup, Sir.

Just. Hiccup? Doctor *Hiccup*, I have known a great many Country Parsons of that Name, especially down in the *Fenns.* Pray where do you live, Sir?

Sir John. Here——and there, Sir.

Just. Why, what a strange Man is this! Where do you preach, Sir? Have you any Cure?

Sir John. Sir——I have——a very good Cure——for a Clap, at your Service.

Just. Lord have mercy upon us!

Sir John. [*Aside.*] This Fellow asks so many impertinent Questions, I believe, I'gad, 'tis the Justice's Wife in the Justice's Clothes.

Just. Mr. Constable, I vow and protest, I don't know what to do with him.

Constab. Truly, he has been but a troublesome Guest to us all Night.

Just. I think, I had e'en best let him go about his Business; for I'm unwilling to expose him.

Constab. E'en what your Worship thinks fit.

Sir John. Sir——not to interrupt Mr. Constable, I have a small Favour to ask.

Just. Sir, I open both my Ears to you.

Sir John. Sir, your very humble Servant. I have a little urgent Business calls upon me; and therefore I desire the Favour of you to bring Matters to a Conclusion.

Just. Sir, if I were sure that Business were not to commit more Disorders, I wou'd release you.

Sir John. None——By my Priesthood!

Just. Then, Mr. Constable, you may discharge him.

Sir John. Sir, your very humble Servant. If you please to accept of a Bottle—

Just. I thank you, kindly, Sir; but I never drink in a Morning. Good-by t'ye, Sir, good-by t'ye.

Sir John. Good by t'ye, good Sir. [*Exit Justice.*] So——now, Mr. Constable, shall you and I go pick up a Whore together?

Constab. No, thank you, Sir; my Wife's enough to satisfy any reasonable Man.

Sir John. [*Aside.*] He, he, he, he—the Fool is married, then. Well, you won't go?

Constab. Not I, truly.

Sir John. Then I'll go by myself; and you and your *Wife* may be damn'd.

[*Exit Sir John.*

Constable. [*Gazing after him.*] Why, God a-mercy, Parson?

[*Exeunt.*

Scene, *Spring-Garden.*

Constant *and* Heartfree *cross the stage. As they go off,* enter Lady Fancyfull *and* Madamoiselle *mask'd, and dogging 'em.*

Const. So; I think we are about the time appointed: let us walk up this way.

[*Exeunt.*

Lady Fan. Good: Thus far I have dogg'd 'em without being discover'd.

'Tis infallibly some Intrigue that brings them to *Spring-Garden*. How my poor Heart is torn and rackt with Fear and Jealousy! Yet let it be any thing but that Flirt *Belinda*, and I'll try to bear it. But if it prove her, all that's Woman in me shall be employ'd to destroy her.

[*Exeunt after Constant and Heartfree.*

Re-enter Constant *and* Heartfree, Lady Fancyfull *and* Madamoiselle *still following at a Distance.*

Const. I see no Females yet, that have any thing to say to us. I'm afraid we are banter'd.

Heart. I wish we were; for I'm in no Humour to make either them or myself merry.

Const. Nay, I'm sure you'll make them merry enough, if I tell 'em why you are dull. But pr'ythee why so heavy and sad before you begin to be ill us'd?

Heart. For the same Reason, perhaps, that you are so brisk and well pleas'd; because both Pains and Pleasures are generally more considerable in Prospect, than when they come to pass.

Enter Lady Brute *and* Belinda, *mask'd and poorly dress'd.*

Const. How now! who are these? Not our Game, I hope.

Heart. If they are, we are e'en well enough serv'd, to come a-hunting here, when we had so much better Game in Chase elsewhere.

Lady Fan. [*To Madamoiselle.*] So, those are their Ladies, without doubt. But I'm afraid that *Doily* Stuff is not worn for want of better Clothes. They are the very Shape and Size of *Belinda* and her Aunt.

Madam. So dey be inteed, Matam.

Lady Fan. We'll slip into this close Arbour, where we may hear all they say.

[*Exeunt Lady Fancyfull and Madamoiselle.*

Lady Brute. What, are you afraid of us, Gentlemen?

Heart. Why, truly, I think we may, if Appearance don't lye.

Bel. Do you always find Women what they appear to be, Sir?

Heart. No, forsooth; but I seldom find 'em better than they appear to be.

Bel. Then the Outside's best, you think?

Heart. 'Tis the honestest.

Const. Have a care, *Heartfree*; you are relapsing again.

Lady Brute. Why, does the Gentleman use to rail at Women?

Const. He has done formerly.

Bel. I suppose he had very good Cause for't. They did not use you so well as you thought you deserv'd, Sir.

Lady Brute. They made themselves merry at your Expence, Sir.

Bel. Laugh'd when you sigh'd——

Lady Brute. Slept while you were waking——

Bel. Had your Porter beat——

Lady Brute. And threw your Billet-doux in the Fire.

Heart. Hey-day, I shall do more than rail presently.

Bel. Why, you won't beat us, will you?

Heart. I don't know but I may.

Const. What the Devil's coming here? Sir *John* in a Gown——And drunk, i'faith.

Enter Sir John.

Sir John. What a Pox——here's *Constant, Heartfree*—and two Whores, I'gad——O you covetous Rogues! what, have you never a spare Punk for your Friend?——But I'll share with you.

[He seizes both the Women.

Heart. Why, what the plague have you been doing, Knight?

Sir John. Why, I have been beating the Watch, and scandalizing the Clergy.

Heart. A very good Account, truly.

64

Sir John. And what do you think I'll do next?

Const. Nay, that no Man can guess.

Sir John. Why, if you'll let me sup with you, I'll treat both your Strumpets.

Lady Brute. [*Aside.*] O Lord, we're undone!

Heart. No, we can't sup together, because we have some Affairs elsewhere. But if you'll accept of these two Ladies, we'll be so complaisant to you, to resign our Right in 'em.

Bel. [*Aside.*] Lord, what shall we do?

Sir John. Let me see; their Clothes are such damn'd Clothes, they won't pawn for the Reckoning.

Heart. Sir John, your Servant. Rapture attend you!

Const. Adieu, Ladies, make much of the Gentleman.

Lady Brute. Why, sure, you won't leave us in the Hands of a drunken Fellow to abuse us.

Sir John. Who do you call a drunken Fellow, you Slut you? I'm a Man of Quality; the King has made me a Knight.

[*Heart. runs off.*

Heart. Ay, ay, you are in good Hands! Adieu, Adieu!

Lady Brute. The Devil's Hands: Let me go, or I'll—For Heaven's sake, protect us!

[*She breaks from him, runs to Constant, twitching off her Mask, and clapping it on again.*

Sir John. I'll Devil you, you Jade you. I'll demolish your ugly Face.

Const. Hold a little, Knight, she swoons.

Sir John. I'll swoon her.

Const. Hey, *Heartfree.*

Re-enter Heartfree. Belinda *runs to him, and shews her face.*

Heart. O Heavens! My dear Creature, stand there a little.

65

Const. Pull him off, *Jack.*

Heart. Hold, mighty Man; look ye, Sir, we did but jest with you. These are Ladies of our Acquaintance that we had a mind to frighten a little, but now you must leave us.

Sir John. Oons, I won't leave you, not I.

Heart. Nay, but you must, though; and therefore make no Words on't.

Sir John. Then you are a couple of damned uncivil Fellows. And I hope your Punks will give you Sauce to your Mutton.

[*Exit Sir John.*

Lady Brute. Oh, I shall never come to myself again, I'm so frightened.

Const. 'Twas a narrow 'Scape, indeed.

Bel. Women must have Frolicks, you see, whatever they cost them.

Heart. This might have proved a dear one, though.

Lady Brute. You are the more obliged to us for the Risk we run upon your Accounts.

Const. And I hope you'll acknowledge something due to our Knight-Errantry, Ladies. This is the second time we have delivered you.

Lady Brute. 'Tis true; and since we see Fate has designed you for our Guardians, 'twill make us the more willing to trust ourselves in your Hands. But you must not have the worse Opinion of us for our innocent Frolick.

Heart. Ladies, you may command our Opinions in every thing that is to your Advantage.

Bel. Then, Sir, I command you to be of Opinion, That Women are sometimes better than they appear to be.

[*Lady Brute and Constant talk apart.*

Heart. Madam, you have made a Convert of me in every thing. I'm grown a Fool: I cou'd be fond of a Woman.

Bel. I thank you, Sir, in the Name of the whole Sex.

Heart. Which Sex nothing but yourself cou'd ever have aton'd for.

Bel. Now has my Vanity a devilish Itch, to know in what my Merit consists.

Heart. In your Humility, Madam, that keeps you ignorant it consists at all.

Bel. One other Compliment, with that serious Face, and I hate you for ever after.

Heart. Some Women love to be abus'd: Is that it you wou'd be at?

Bel. No, not that, neither: But I'd have Men talk plainly what's fit for Women to hear; without putting 'em either to a real or an affected Blush.

Heart. Why, then, in as plain Terms as I can find to express myself, I could love you even to—Matrimony itself a'most, I'gad.

Bel. Just as Sir *John* did her Ladyship there.——What think you? Don't you believe one Month's time might bring you down to the same Indifference, only clad in a little better Manners, perhaps? Well, you Men are unaccountable things, mad till you have your Mistresses, and then stark mad till you are rid of 'em again. Tell me honestly, Is not your Patience put to a much severer Trial after Possession than before?

Heart. With a great many I must confess it is, to our eternal Scandal; but I——dear Creature, do but try me.

Bel. That's the surest way, indeed, to know, but not the safest. [*To Lady Brute.*] Madam, are not you for taking a Turn in the Great Walk? It's almost dark, no body will know us.

Lady Brute. Really I find myself something idle, *Belinda*: besides, I doat upon this little odd private Corner. But don't let my lazy Fancy confine you. [*Const. aside.*] So, she wou'd be left alone with me; that's well.

Bel. Well, we'll take one Turn, and come to you again. [*To Heart.*] Come, Sir, shall we go pry into the Secrets of the Garden? Who knows what Discoveries we may make?

Heart. Madam, I'm at your Service.

Const. [*To Heart. aside.*] Don't make too much haste back; for, d'ye hear?——I may be busy.

Heart. Enough.

Lady Brute. Sure you think me scandalously free, Mr. *Constant.* I'm afraid I shall lose your good Opinion of me.

Const. My good Opinion, Madam, is like your Cruelty——ne'er to be remov'd.

Lady Brute. But if I should remove my Cruelty, then there's an end of your good Opinion.

Const. There is not so strict an Alliance between 'em, neither. 'Tis certain I shou'd love you then better (if that be possible) than I do now; and where I love, I always esteem.

Lady Brute. Indeed, I doubt you much. Why, suppose you had a Wife, and she should entertain a Gallant?

Const. If I gave her just Cause, how cou'd I justly condemn her?

Lady Brute. Ah! but you'd differ widely about just Causes.

Const. But Blows can bear no Dispute.

Lady Brute. Nor ill Manners much, truly.

Const. Then no Woman upon Earth has so just a Cause as you have.

Lady Brute. O, but a faithful Wife is a beautiful Character.

Const. To a deserving Husband, I confess it is.

Lady Brute. But can his Faults release my Duty?

Const. In Equity, without doubt. And where Laws dispense with Equity, Equity should dispense with Laws.

Lady Brute. Pray let's leave this Dispute; for you Men have as much Witchcraft in your Arguments, as Women have in their Eyes.

Const. But whilst you attack me with your Charms, 'tis but reasonable I assault you with mine.

Lady Brute. The Case is not the same. What Mischief we do, we can't help, and therefore are to be forgiven.

Const. Beauty soon obtains Pardon for the Pain that it gives, when it applies the Balm of Compassion to the Wound: But a fine Face, and a hard Heart, is almost as bad as an ugly Face and a soft one; both very troublesome to many a poor Gentleman.

Lady Brute. Yes, and to many a poor Gentlewoman, too, I can assure you. But pray, which of 'em is it that most afflicts you?

Const. Your Glass and Conscience will inform you, Madam. But for Heaven's sake (for now I must be serious), if Pity, or if Gratitude can move you; [*Taking her Hand.*] if Constancy and Truth have power to tempt you; if Love, if Adoration can affect you; give me at least some Hopes, that Time may do what you perhaps mean never to perform; 'twill ease my Sufferings, tho' not quench my Flame.

Lady Brute. Your Sufferings eas'd, your Flame wou'd soon abate: And that I would preserve, not quench it, Sir.

Const. Wou'd you preserve it, nourish it with Favours; for that's the Food it naturally requires.

Lady Brute. Yet on that natural Food 'twould surfeit soon, shou'd I resolve to grant all you wou'd ask.

Const. And in refusing all, you starve it. Forgive me, therefore, since my Hunger rages, if I at last grow wild, and in my frenzy force at least this from you. [*Kissing her Hand.*] Or if you'd have my Flame soar higher still, then grant me this, and this, and Thousands more; [*Kissing first her Hand, then her Neck.*] [*Aside.*] For now's the time she melts into Compassion.

Lady Brute. [*Aside.*] Poor Coward Virtue, how it shuns the Battle! O Heavens! let me go.

Const. Ay, go, ay: Where shall we go, my charming Angel——into this private Arbour——Nay, let's lose no time——Moments are precious.

Lady Brute. And Lovers wild. Pray let us stop here; at least for this time.

Const. 'Tis impossible; he that has power over you, can have none over himself.

As he is forcing her into the arbour, Lady Fancyfull *and* Madamoiselle *bolt out upon them, and run over the stage.*

Lady Brute. Ah! I'm lost!

Lady Fan. Fe, fe, fe, fe, fe.

Madam. Fe, fe, fe, fe, fe.

Const. Death and Furies, who are these?

Lady Brute. O Heavens! I'm out of my Wits; if they knew me, I am ruin'd.

Const. Don't be frightened: Ten thousand to one they are Strangers to you.

Lady Brute. Whatever they are, I won't stay here a Moment longer.

Const. Whither will you go?

Lady Brute. Home, as if the Devil were in me. Lord, where's this *Belinda* now?

Enter Belinda *and* Heartfree.

O! 'tis well you are come: I'm so frightened, my Hair stands an end. Let's be gone, for Heaven's sake!

Bel. Lord, what's the matter?

Lady Brute. The Devil's the Matter; we are discovered. Here's a couple of Women have done the most impertinent thing. Away, away, away, away, away.

[Exit running.

Re-enter Lady Fancyfull *and* Madamoiselle.

Lady Fan. Well, *Madamoiselle*, 'tis a prodigious thing how Women can suffer filthy Fellows to grow so familiar with 'em.

Madam. Ah Madame, *il n'y a rien de si naturel.*

Lady Fan. Fe, fe, fe! But, oh my Heart! O Jealousy! O Torture! I'm upon the rack. What shall I do? My Lover's lost, I ne'er shall see him mine. [*Pausing.*]——But I may be reveng'd; and that's the same thing. Ah sweet Revenge! Thou welcome Thought, thou healing Balsam to my wounded Soul! Be but propitious on this one Occasion, I'll place my Heaven in thee, for all my Life to come.

To Woman how indulgent Nature's kind!
No Blast of Fortune long disturbs her Mind:
Compliance to her Fate supports her still;

70

If Love won't make her happy—Mischief will.

[*Exeunt.*

ACT V.

Scene, Lady Fancyfull's *House.*

Enter Lady Fancyfull *and* Madamoiselle.

Lady Fan. Well, *Madamoiselle,* did you dog the filthy Things?

Madam. O que ouy, Madame.

Lady Fan. And where are they?

Madam. Au Logis.

Lady Fan. What, Men and all?

Madam. Tous ensemble.

Lady Fan. O Confidence! What, carry their Fellows to their own House?

Madam. C'est que le Mari n'y est pas.

Lady Fan. No; so I believe, truly. But he shall be there, and quickly too, if I can find him out. Well, 'tis a prodigious thing, to see when Men and Women get together, how they fortify one another in their Impudence. But if that drunken Fool, her Husband, he to be found in e'er a Tavern in Town, I'll send him amongst 'em: I'll spoil their sport.

Madam. En verité, Madame, *ce seroit domage.*

Lady Fan. 'Tis in vain to oppose it, *Madamoiselle;* therefore never go about it. For I am the steadiest Creature in the World—when I have determin'd to do Mischief. So, come along.

[*Exeunt.*

Scene, Sir John Brute's *House.*

Enter Constant, Heartfree, Lady Brute, Belinda, *and* Lovewell.

Lady Brute. But are you sure you don't mistake, *Lovewell?*

Lov. Madam, I saw 'em all go into the Tavern together, and my Master was so drunk he cou'd scarce stand.

Lady Brute. Then, Gentlemen, I believe we may venture to let you stay,

73

and play at Cards with us, an Hour or two: For they'll scarce part till Morning.

Bel. I think 'tis pity they should ever part.

Const. The Company that's here, Madam.

Lady Brute. Then, Sir, the Company that's here must remember to part itself in time.

Const. Madam, we don't intend to forfeit your future Favours by an indiscreet Usage of this. The Moment you give us the Signal, we shan't fail to make our Retreat.

Lady Brute. Upon those Conditions, then, let us sit down to Cards.

Enter Lovewell.

Lov. O Lord, Madam, here's my Master just staggering in upon you; he has been quarrelsome yonder, and they have kick'd him out of the Company.

Lady Brute. Into the Closet, Gentlemen, for Heaven's sake; I'll wheedle him to Bed, if possible.

[*Const. and Heart. run into the Closet.*

Enter Sir John, *all dirt and bloody.*

Lady Brute. Ah——Ah——he's all over Blood!

Sir John. What the plague does the Woman—squall for? Did you never see a Man in Pickle before?

Lady Brute. Lord, where have you been?

Sir John. I have been at——Cuffs.

Lady Brute. I fear that is not all. I hope you are not wounded.

Sir John. Sound as a Roach, Wife.

Lady Brute. I'm mighty glad to hear it.

Sir John. You know—I think you lye.

Lady Brute. You do me wrong to think so. For Heaven's my Witness; I had rather see my own Blood trickle down, than yours.

Sir John. Then will I be crucify'd.

Lady Brute. 'Tis a hard Fate, I shou'd not be believ'd.

Sir John. 'Tis a damn'd Atheistical Age, Wife.

Lady Brute. I am sure I have given you a thousand tender Proofs, how great my Care is of you. But, spite of all your cruel Thoughts, I'll still persist, and at this Moment, if I can, persuade you to lie down and sleep a little.

Sir John. Why—do you think I am drunk—you Slut, you?

Lady Brute. Heaven forbid I shou'd! But I'm afraid you are feverish. Pray let me feel your Pulse.

Sir John. Stand off, and be damn'd.

Lady Brute. Why, I see your Distemper in your very Eyes. You are all on Fire. Pray, go to Bed; let me intreat you.

Sir John.——Come, kiss me, then.

Lady Brute. [*Kissing him.*] There: Now go. [*Aside.*] He stinks like Poison.

Sir John. I see it goes damnably against your Stomach—And therefore —Kiss me again.

Lady Brute. Nay, now you fool me.

Sir John. Do't, I say.

Lady Brute. [*Aside.*] Ah, Lord have mercy upon me! Well—there: now will you go?

Sir John. Now, Wife, you shall see my Gratitude. You gave me two Kisses—I'll give you—two hundred.

[*Kisses, and tumbles her.*

Lady Brute. O Lord! Pray, Sir John, be quiet. Heavens, what a Pickle am I in!

Bel. [*Aside.*] If I were in her Pickle, I'd call my Gallant out of the Closet, and he shou'd cudgel him soundly.

Sir John. So, now you being as dirty and as nasty as myself, we may go

75

pig together. But first I must have a Cup of your cold Tea, Wife.

[*Going to the Closet.*

Lady Brute. O I'm ruin'd! There's none there, my Dear.

Sir John. I'll warrant you I'll find some, my Dear.

Lady Brute. You can't open the Door, the Lock's spoil'd; I have been turning and turning the Key this half Hour to no purpose. I'll send for the Smith to-morrow.

Sir John. There's ne'er a Smith in *Europe* can open a Door with more Expedition than I can do——As for Example—Poh! [*He bursts open the Door with his Foot.*]——How now! What the Devil have we got here? ——Constant——Heartfree——And two Whores again, I'gad—— This is the worst cold Tea——that ever I met with in my Life——

Enter Constant *and* Heartfree.

Lady Brute. [*Aside.*] O Lord, what will become of us?

Sir John. Gentlemen——I am your very humble Servant—I give you many Thanks——I see you take Care of my Family——I shall do all I can to return the Obligation.

Const. Sir, how oddly soever this Business may appear to you, you would have no cause to be uneasy, if you knew the Truth of all things; your Lady is the most virtuous Woman in the World, and nothing has past but an innocent Frolick.

Heart. Nothing else, upon my Honour, Sir.

Sir John. You are both very civil Gentlemen—And my Wife, there, is a very civil Gentlewoman; therefore I don't doubt but many civil things have past between you. Your very humble Servant.

Lady Brute. [*Aside to Const.*] Pray be gone: He's so drunk he can't hurt us to-night, and to-morrow Morning you shall hear from us.

Const. I'll obey you, Madam. Sir, when you are cool, you'll understand Reason better. So then I shall take the pains to inform you. If not——I wear a Sword, Sir, and so good by t'ye. Come along, *Heartfree.*

[*Exit.*

Sir John. Wear a Sword, Sir—And what of all that, Sir? He comes to my

House; eats my Meat; lies with my Wife; dishonours my Family; gets a Bastard to inherit my Estate——And when I ask a civil Account of all this—Sir, says he, I wear a Sword—Wear a Sword, Sir? Yes, Sir, says he, I wear a Sword——It may be a good Answer at Cross-purposes; but 'tis a damn'd one to a Man in my whimsical Circumstance——Sir, says he, I wear a Sword! [*To Lady Brute.*] And what do you wear now? ha! tell me. [*Sitting down in a great Chair.*] What, you are modest, and can't— Why, then, I'll tell you, you Slut, you. You wear——an impudent, lewd Face——A damn'd designing Heart——And a Tail——and a Tail full of——[*He falls fast asleep, snoaring.*]

Lady Brute. So; thanks to kind Heaven, he's fast for some Hours.

Bel. 'Tis well he is so, that we may have time to lay our Story handsomely; for we must lye like the Devil, to bring ourselves off.

Lady Brute. What shall we say, *Belinda?*

Bel. [*Musing.*]——I'll tell you: It must all light upon *Heartfree* and I. We'll say he has courted me some time, but, for Reasons unknown to us, has ever been very earnest the thing might be kept from Sir *John.* That therefore hearing him upon the Stairs, he ran into the Closet, tho' against our Will, and *Constant* with him, to prevent Jealousy. And to give this a good impudent Face of Truth, (that I may deliver you from the trouble you are in) I'll e'en, if he pleases, marry him.

Lady Brute. I'm beholden to you, Cousin; but that wou'd be carrying the Jest a little too far for your own sake: You know he's a younger Brother, and has nothing.

Bel. 'Tis true: But I like him, and have Fortune enough to keep above Extremity: I can't say I would live with him in a Cell, upon Love and Bread and Butter: But I had rather have the Man I love, and a middle State of Life, than that Gentleman in the Chair there, and twice your Ladyship's Splendour.

Lady Brute. In truth, Niece, you are in the right on't; for I am very uneasy with my Ambition. But, perhaps, had I married as you'll do, I might have been as ill us'd.

Bel. Some Risk, I do confess, there always is: But if a Man has the least Spark either of Honour or Good-nature, he can never use a Woman ill, that loves him, and makes his Fortune both. Yet I must own to you, some little struggling I still have with this teazing Ambition of ours; for Pride, you know, is as natural to a Woman, as 'tis to a Saint. I can't help being fond of this Rogue; and yet it goes to my Heart, to think I must never whisk to *Hyde-Park* with above a Pair of Horses; have no Coronet upon my Coach, nor a Page to carry up my Train. But above all—that Business of Place—Well, taking place is a noble Prerogative—

Lady Brute. Especially after a Quarrel—

Bel. Or of a Rival. But pray say no more on't, for fear I change my Mind; for, o' my Conscience, wer't not for your Affair in the Balance, I should go near to pick up some odious Man of Quality yet, and only take poor *Heartfree* for a Gallant.

Lady Brute. Then him you must have, however things go?

Bel. Yes.

Lady Brute. Why, we may pretend what we will: but 'tis a hard matter to live without the Man we love.

Bel. Especially when we are married to the Man we hate. Pray tell me: Do the Men of the Town ever believe us virtuous, when they see us do so?

Lady Brute. O, no: Nor indeed, hardly, let us do what we will. The most of them think, there is no such thing as Virtue, consider'd in the strictest Notions of it; and therefore when you hear 'em say, such a one is a Woman of Reputation, they only mean she's a Woman of Discretion. For they consider we have no more Religion than they have, nor so much Morality; and between you and I, *Belinda,* I'm afraid the want of Inclination seldom protects any of us.

Bel. But what think you of the Fear of being found out?

Lady Brute. I think That never kept any Woman virtuous long. We are not such Cowards, neither. No: Let us once pass Fifteen, and we have too good an Opinion of our own Cunning, to believe the World can penetrate into what we would keep a Secret. And so, in short, we cannot reasonably blame the Men for judging of us by themselves.

Bel. But sure we are not so wicked as they are, after all?

Lady Brute. We are as wicked, Child, but our Vice lies another way: Men have more Courage than we, so they commit more bold, impudent Sins. They quarrel, fight, swear, drink, blaspheme, and the like: Whereas we, being Cowards, only backbite, tell Lyes, cheat at Cards, and so forth. But 'tis late: Let's end our Discourse for to-night, and, out of an excess of Charity, take a small Care of that nasty, drunken Thing there——Do but look at him, *Belinda!*

Bel. Ah——'tis a savoury Dish.

Lady Brute. As savoury as 'tis, I'm cloy'd with't. Pr'ythee call the Butler to take it away.

Bel. Call the Butler!—--Call the Scavenger! [*To a Servant within.*] Who's there? Call *Rasor!* Let him take away his Master, scour him clean with a little Sope and Sand, and so put him to Bed.

Lady Brute. Come, *Belinda*, I'll e'en lie with you to-night; and in the Morning we'll send for our Gentlemen to set this Matter even.

Bel. With all my Heart.

Lady Brute. Good Night, my Dear.

[*Making a low Curtsy to Sir John.*

[*Both.*] Ha, ha, ha!

[*Exeunt.*

Enter Rasor.

Rasor. My Lady there's a Wag—My Master there's a Cuckold. Marriage is a slippery thing—Women have depraved Appetites.—My Lady's a Wag; I have heard all; I have seen all; I understand all; and I'll tell all; for my little *French-woman* loves News dearly. This Story'll gain her Heart, or nothing will. [*To his Master.*] Come, Sir, your Head's too full of Fumes at present, to make room for your Jealousy; but I reckon we shall have rare work with you, when your Pate's empty. Come to your Kennel, you cuckoldly, drunken Sot, you!

[*Carries him out upon his Back.*

Scene, Lady Fancyfull's *House.*

Enter Lady Fancyfull *and* Madamoiselle.

Lady Fan. But, why did not you tell me before, *Madamoiselle*, that *Rasor* and you were fond?

Madam. De Modesty hinder me, Matam.

Lady Fan. Why, truly, Modesty does often hinder us from doing things
79

we have an extravagant mind to. But does he love you well enough yet, to do any thing you bid him? Do you think, to oblige you, he wou'd speak Scandal?

Madam. Matam, to oblige your Ladyship, he shall speak Blasphemy.

Lady Fan. Why, then, *Madamoiselle*, I'll tell you what you shall do. You shall engage him to tell his Master all that past at *Spring Garden*: I have a mind he shou'd know what a Wife and a Niece he has got.

Madam. Il le fera, Madame.

Enter a Footman, *who speaks to* Madamoiselle *apart.*

Foot. Madamoiselle, yonder's Mr. *Rasor* desires to speak with you.

Madam. Tell him, I come presently. [*Exit Footman.*] *Rasor* be dare, Matam.

Lady Fan. That's fortunate. Well, I'll leave you together. And if you find him stubborn, *Madamoiselle*—hark you—don't refuse him a few little reasonable Liberties to put him into Humour.

Madam. Laissez moy faire.

[*Exit Lady Fancyfull.*

[*Rasor* peeps in; and seeing Lady *Fancyfull* gone, runs to *Madamoiselle,* takes her about the Neck, and kisses her.

Madam. How now, Confidence?

Rasor. How now, Modesty!

Madam. Who make you so familiar, Sirrah?

Rasor. My Impudence, Hussy.

Madam. Stand off, Rogue-Face.

Rasor. Ah——*Madamoiselle*——great News at our House.

Madam. Why, vat be de matter?

Rasor. The Matter?—Why, Uptails All's the Matter.

Madam. Tu te mocque de moy.

Rasor. Now do you long to know the Particulars: The Time when—The

Place where—The Manner how. But I don't tell you a Word more.

Madam. Nay, den dou kill me, *Rasor.*

Rasor. Come, kiss me, then.

> [*Clapping his Hands behind him.*

Madam. Nay, pridee tell me.

Rasor. Good by t' ye.

> [*Going.*

Madam. Hold, hold: I will kiss dee.

> [*Kissing him.*

Rasor. So, that's civil: Why, now, my pretty Poll, my Goldfinch, my little Waterwagtail——you must know, that——Come, kiss me again.

Madam. I won't kiss de no more.

Rasor. Good by t' ye.

> [*Going.*

Madam. Doucement! *Derre: es tu content?*

> [*Kissing him.*

Rasor. So: Now I'll tell thee all. Why, the News is, That Cuckoldom in Folio is newly printed; and Matrimony in Quarto is just going into the Press. Will you buy any Books, *Madamoiselle?*

Madam. Tu parle comme un Libraire; de Devil no understand dee.

Rasor. Why, then, that I may make myself intelligible to a Waiting-Woman, I'll speak like a Valet de Chambre. My Lady has cuckolded my Master.

Madam. Bon.

Rasor. Which we take very ill from her Hands, I can tell her that. We can't yet prove Matter of Fact upon her.

Madam. N'importe.

Rasor. But we can prove, that Matter of Fact had like to have been upon her.

Madam. Ouy da.

Rasor. For we have such bloody Circumstances—

Madam. Sans doute.

Rasor. That any Man of Parts may draw tickling Conclusions from 'em.

Madam. Fort bien.

Rasor. We found a couple of tight, well-built Gentlemen stufft into her Ladyship's Closet.

Madam. Le Diable!

Rasor. And I, in my particular Person, have discovered a most damnable Plot, how to persuade my poor Master, that all this Hide and Seek, this *Will* in the *Whisp,* has no other meaning than a Christian Marriage for sweet Mrs. *Belinda.*

Madam. Une Mariage?——*Ah les Droles!*

Rasor. Don't you interrupt me, Hussy; 'tis agreed, I say. And my innocent Lady, to wriggle herself out at the Back-door of the Business, turns Marriage-Bawd to her Niece, and resolves to deliver up her fair Body to be tumbled and mumbled by that young liquorish Whipster, *Heartfree.* Now are you satisfy'd?

Madam. No.

Rasor. Right Woman; always gaping for more.

Madam. Dis be all, den, dat dou know?

Rasor. All? Aye, and a great deal, too, I think.

Madam. Dou be Fool, dou know noting. *Ecoute, mon pauvre* Rasor. Dou sees des two Eyes?—Des two Eyes have see de Devil.

Rasor. The Woman's mad.

Madam. In *Spring-Garden,* dat Rogue *Constant* meet dy Lady.

Rasor. Bon.

Madam.——I'll tell dee no more.

Rasor. Nay, pr'ythee, my Swan.

Madam. Come, kiss me den.

> [*Clapping her Hands behind her as he did before.*

Rasor. I won't kiss you, not I.

Madam. Adieu.

> [*Going.*

Rasor. Hold——Now proceed.

> [*Gives her a hearty Kiss.*

Madam. A ça——I hide myself in one cunning Place, where I hear all, and see all. First, dy drunken Master come *mal a propos*; but de Sot no know his own dear Wife, so he leave her to her Sport—Den de Game begin. De Lover say soft ting: De Lady look upon de Ground. [*As she speaks, Rasor still acts the Man, and she the Woman.*] He take her by de Hand: She turn her Head on oder Way. Den he squeeze very hard: Den she pull——very softly. Den he take her in his Arm: Den she give him leetel pat. Den he kiss her Tettons. Den she say—Pish, nay see. Den he tremble: Den she—sigh. Den he pull her into de Arbour: Den she pinch him.

Rasor. Aye, but not so hard, you Baggage, you.

Madam. Den he grow bold: She grow weak, he tro her down, *il tombe dessu, le Diable assiste, il emport tout.* [*Rasor struggles with her, as if he would throw her down.*] Stand off, Sirrah!

Rasor. You have set me a-fire, you Jade, you.

Madam. Den go to de River, and quench dy self.

Rasor. What an unnatural Harlot 'tis!

Madam. Rasor.

> [*Looking languishingly on him.*

Rasor. Madamoiselle.

Madam. Dou no love me.

Rasor. Not love thee?—More than a *Frenchman* does Soup.

83

Madam. Den dou will refuse nothing dat I bid dee?

Rasor. Don't bid me be damn'd, then.

Madam. No, only tell dy Master all I have tell dee of dy Laty.

Rasor. Why, you little, malicious Strumpet, you, shou'd you like to be serv'd so?

Madam. Dou dispute den?—Adieu.

Rasor. Hold—But why wilt thou make me such a Rogue, my Dear?

Madam. Voila un vrai Anglois! Il est amoureux, et cependant il veut raisonner. Va t'en au Diable.

Rasor. Hold once more: In hopes thou'lt give me up thy Body, I resign thee my Soul.

Madam. Bon, ecoute donc;——If dou fail me——I never see de more ——If dou obey me——*Je m'abandonne a toy.* [*She takes him about the Neck, and gives him a smacking Kiss.*]

[*Exit Madamoiselle.*

Rasor. [*Licking his Lips.*] Not be a Rogue?——*Amor vincit Omnia.*

[*Exit Rasor.*

Enter Lady Fancyfull *and* Madamoiselle.

Lady Fan. Marry, say ye? Will the two Things marry?

Madam. On le va faire, Madame.

Lady Fan. Look you, *Madamoiselle*—In short, I can't bear it——No; I find I can't—If once I see 'em a-bed together, I shall have ten thousand Thoughts in my Head will make me run distracted. Therefore run and call *Rasor* back immediately; for something must be done to stop this impertinent Wedding. If I can but defer it four-and-twenty Hours, I'll make such Work about Town, with that little pert Slut's Reputation, he shall as soon marry a Witch.

Madam. [*Aside.*] *La voilà bien intentionnée.*

[*Exeunt.*

Scene, Constant's Lodgings.

84

Enter Constant *and* Heartfree.

Const. But what dost think will become of this Business?

Heart. 'Tis easier to think what will not come on't.

Const. What's that?

Heart. A Challenge. I know the Knight too well for that; his dear Body will always prevail upon his noble Soul to be quiet.

Const. But tho' he dare not challenge me, perhaps he may venture to challenge his Wife.

Heart. Not if you whisper him in the Ear, you won't have him do't; and there's no other way left, that I see. For as drunk as he was, he'll remember you and I were where we shou'd not be; and I don't think him quite Blockhead enough yet to be persuaded we were got into his Wife's Closet only to peep into her Prayer-Book.

Enter a Servant *with a letter.*

Serv. Sir, here's a Letter; a Porter brought it.

Const. O ho, here's Instructions for us.

Reads:

The Accident that has happen'd has touch'd our Invention to the quick we wou'd fain come off, without your help; but find that's impossible. In a Word, the whole Business must be thrown upon a matrimonial intrigue between your friend and mine. But if the parties are not fond enough to go quite through with the matter, 'Tis sufficient for our turn, they own the design. We'll find pretences enough to break the match.

Adieu.

—Well, Woman for Invention! How long wou'd my Block-Head have been producing this!——-Hey, *Heartfree?* What, musing, Man? Pr'ythee be chearful. What say'st thou, Friend, to this matrimonial Remedy?

Heart. Why, I say, 'tis worse than the Disease.

Const. Here's a Fellow for you! There's Beauty and Money on her Side, and Love up to the Ears on his: and yet——

Heart. And yet, I think, I may reasonably be allow'd to boggle at

85

marrying the Niece, in the very Moment that you are debauching the Aunt.

Const. Why, truly, there may be something in that. But have not you a good Opinion enough of your own Parts, to believe you cou'd keep a Wife to yourself?

Heart. I shou'd have, if I had a good Opinion enough of her's, to believe she cou'd do as much by me. For to do 'em right, after all, the Wife seldom rambles, till the Husband shews her the way.

Const. 'Tis true, a Man of real Worth scarce ever is a Cuckold, but by his own Fault. Women are not naturally lewd; there must be something to urge 'em to it. They'll cuckold a Churl, out of Revenge; a Fool, because they despise him; a Beast, because they loath him. But when they make bold with a Man they once had a well-grounded Value for, 'tis because they first see themselves neglected by him.

Heart. Nay, were I well assured that I should never grow Sir *John,* I ne'er shou'd fear *Belinda,* wou'd play my Lady. But our Weakness, thou knowest, my Friend, consists in that very Change we so impudently throw upon (indeed) a steadier and more generous Sex.

Const. Why, 'faith, we are a little impudent in that matter, that's the truth on't. But this is wonderful, to see you grown so warm an Advocate for those whom (but t'other Day) you took so much Pains to abuse.

Heart. All Revolutions run into Extremes; the Bigot makes the boldest Atheist; and the coyest Saint, the most extravagant Strumpet. But, pr'ythee, advise me in this Good and Evil, this Life and Death, this Blessing and Cursing, that's set before me. Shall I marry, or die a Maid?

Const. Why, 'faith, *Heartfree,* Matrimony is like an Army going to engage. Love's the forlorn Hope, which is soon cut off; the Marriage-Knot is the main Body, which may stand buff a long, long time; and Repentance is the Rear-Guard, which rarely gives ground as long as the main Body has a Being.

Heart. Conclusion, then; you advise me to whore on, as you do.

Const. That's not concluded yet. For tho' Marriage be a Lottery, in which there are a wondrous many Blanks; yet there is one inestimable Lot, in which the only Heaven on Earth is written. Wou'd your kind Fate but guide your Hand to that, tho' I were wrapt in all that Luxury itself could clothe me with, I still shou'd envy you.

Heart. And justly, too; for to be capable of loving one, doubtless, is better than to possess a thousand. But how far that Capacity's in me, alas! I know not.

Const. But you wou'd know.

Heart. I wou'd so.

Const. Matrimony will inform you. Come, one Flight of Resolution carries you to the Land of Experience; where, in a very moderate time, you'll know the Capacity of your Soul and your Body both, or I'm mistaken.

[Exeunt.

Scene, Sir John Brute's House.

Enter Lady Brute and Belinda.

Bel. Well, Madam, what Answer have you from 'em?

Lady Brute. That they'll be here this Moment. I fancy 'twill end in a Wedding: I'm sure he's a Fool if it don't. Ten thousand Pounds, and such a Lass as you are, is no contemptible Offer to a younger Brother. But are not you under strange Agitations? Pr'ythee, how does your Pulse beat?

Bel. High and low, I have much ado to be valiant: sure it must feel very strange to go to Bed to a Man?

Lady Brute. Um——it does feel a little odd at first; but it will soon grow easy to you.

Enter Constant and Heartfree.

Lady Brute. Good-morrow, Gentlemen: How have you slept after your Adventure?

Heart. Some careful Thoughts, Ladies, on your accounts, have kept us waking.

Bel. And some careful Thoughts on your own, I believe, have hindered you from sleeping. Pray how does this matrimonial Project relish with you?

Heart. Why, 'faith, e'en as storming Towns does with Soldiers, where the Hope of delicious Plunder banishes the Fear of being knock'd on the Head.

Bel. Is it then possible, after all, that you dare think of downright lawful Wedlock?

Heart. Madam, you have made me so fool-hardy, I dare do any thing.

Bel. Then, Sir, I challenge you; and Matrimony's the Spot where I expect you.

Heart. 'Tis enough; I'll not fail. [*Aside.*] So, now, I am in for *Hobbes's Voyage*; a great Leap in the Dark.

Lady Brute. Well, Gentlemen, this Matter being concluded then, have you got your Lessons ready? for Sir *John* is grown such an Atheist of late, he'll believe nothing upon easy Terms.

Const. We'll find ways to extend his Faith, Madam. But pray how do you find him this Morning?

Lady Brute. Most lamentably morose, chewing the Cud after last Night's Discovery, of which, however, he had but a confus'd Notion e'en now. But I'm afraid the Valet de Chambre has told him all; for they are very busy together at this Moment. When I told him of *Belinda's Marriage*, I had no other Answer but a Grunt: From which, you may draw what Conclusions you think fit. But to your Notes, Gentlemen, he's here.

Enter Sir John *and* Rasor.

Const. Good-morrow, Sir.

Heart. Good-morrow, Sir *John*; I'm very sorry my Indiscretion shou'd cause so much Disorder in your Family.

Sir John. Disorders generally come from Indiscretion, Sir; 'tis no strange thing at all.

Lady Brute. I hope, my Dear, you are satisfied there was no wrong intended you.

Sir John. None, my Dove.

Bel. If not, I hope my Consent to marry Mr. *Heartfree* will convince you. For as little as I know of Amours, Sir, I can assure you, one

88

Intrigue is enough to bring four People together, without further Mischief.

Sir John. And I know too, that Intrigues tend to Procreation of more kinds than one. One Intrigue will beget another, as soon as beget a Son or a Daughter.

Const. I am very sorry, Sir, to see you still seem unsatisfy'd with a Lady, whose more than common Virtue, I am sure were she my Wife, shou'd meet a better Usage.

Sir John. Sir, if her Conduct has put a Trick upon her Virtue, her Virtue's the Bubble, but her Husband's the Loser.

Const. Sir, you have receiv'd a sufficient Answer already, to justify both her Conduct and mine. You'll pardon me for meddling in your Family-affairs; but I perceive I am the Man you are jealous of, and therefore it concerns me.

Sir John. Wou'd it did not concern me, and then I shou'd not care who it concern'd.

Const. Well, Sir, if Truth and Reason won't content you, I know but one way more, which, if you think fit, you may take.

Sir John. Lord, Sir, you are very hasty! If I had been found at Prayers in your Wife's Closet, I should have allow'd you twice as much time to come to yourself in.

Const. Nay, Sir, if Time be all you want, we have no Quarrel.

Heart. I told you how the Sword wou'd work upon him.

[*Sir John muses.*

Const. Let him muse; however, I'll lay fifty Pound our Foreman brings us in, Not Guilty.

Sir John. [*Aside.*] 'Tis well——'tis very well——In spite of that young Jade's matrimonial Intrigue, I am a downright stinking Cuckold—— Here they are——Boo——[*Putting his hand to his Forehead.*] Methinks, I could butt with a Bull. What the Plague did I marry her for? I knew she did not like me; if she had, she wou'd have lain with me; for I wou'd have done so, because I lik'd her; but that's past, and I have her. And now, what shall I do with her?——If I put my Horns into my Pocket, she'll grow insolent——if I don't, that Goat there, that

Stallion, is ready to whip me thro' the Guts.—The Debate then is reduced to this: Shall I die a Hero, or live a Rascal?——Why, wiser Men than I have long since concluded, that a living Dog is better than a dead Lion.——[*To Const. and Heart.*] Gentlemen, now my Wine and my Passion are governable, I must own, I have never observ'd any Thing in my Wife's Course of Life, to back me in my Jealousy of her: But Jealousy's a Mark of Love; so she need not trouble her Head about it, as long as I make no more Words on't.

Lady Fancyfull enters disguis'd, and addresses to Belinda *apart.*

Const. I'm glad to see your Reason rule at last. Give me your Hand: I hope you'll look upon me as you are wont.

Sir John. Your humble Servant. [*Aside.*] A wheedling Son of a Whore!

Heart. And that I may be sure you are Friends with me, too, pray give me your Consent to wed your Niece.

Sir John. Sir, you have it with all my Heart: Damn me if you han't. [*Aside.*] 'Tis time to get rid of her: A young, pert Pimp; she'll make an incomparable Bawd in a little time.

Enter a Servant, *who gives* Heartfree *a letter.*

Bel. Heartfree your Husband, say you? 'Tis impossible.

Lady Fan. Wou'd to kind Heaven it were! But 'tis too true; and in the World there lives not such a Wretch. I'm young; and either I have been flatter'd by my Friends, as well as Glass, or Nature has been kind and generous to me. I had a Fortune, too, was greater far than he could ever hope for; but with my Heart I am robb'd of all the rest. I am slighted and I'm beggar'd both at once: I have scarce a bare Subsistence from the Villain, yet dare complain to none; for he has sworn if e'er 'tis known I'm his Wife, he'll murder me.

[*Weeping.*

Bel. The Traitor!

Lady Fan. I accidentally was told he courted you: Charity soon prevail'd upon me to prevent your Misery: And, as you see, I'm still so generous even to him, as not to suffer he should do a thing for which the Law might take away his Life.

[*Weeping.*

Bel. Poor Creature! how I pity her!

[*They continue talking aside.*

Heart. [*Aside.*] Death and Damnation!——-Let me read it again. [*Reads.*] Tho' I have a particular reason not to let you know who I am till I see you; yet you'll easily believe 'tis a faithful Friend that gives you this Advice. I have lain with *Belinda* (Good!)—I have a Child by her (Better and better!) which is now at Nurse; (Heaven be prais'd) and I think the Foundation laid for another: (Ha!—*Old Truepenny!*)—No Rack cou'd have tortur'd this Story from me; but Friendship has done it. I heard of your Design to marry her, and cou'd not see you abus'd. Make use of my Advice, but keep my Secret till I ask you for't again. Adieu.

[*Exit Lady Fancyfull.*

Const. [*To Bel.*] Come, Madam, shall we send for the Parson? I doubt here's no Business for the Lawyer: Younger Brothers have nothing to settle but their Hearts, and that I believe my Friend here has already done very faithfully.

Bel. [*Scornfully.*] Are you sure, Sir, there are no old Mortgages upon it?

Heart. [*Coldly.*] If you think there are, Madam, it mayn't be amiss to defer the Marriage till you are sure they are paid off.

Bel. [*Aside.*] How the gall'd Horse kicks!

[*To Heart.*] We'll defer it as long as you please, Sir.

Heart. The more time we take to consider on't, Madam, the less apt we shall be to commit Oversights; therefore, if you please, we will put it off for just nine Months.

Bel. Guilty Consciences make Men Cowards; I don't wonder you want time to resolve.

Heart. And they make Women desperate; I don't wonder you are so quickly determin'd.

Bel. What does the Fellow mean?

Heart. What does the Lady mean?

Sir John. Zoons, what do you both mean?

[*Heart. and Bel. walk chasing about.*

91

Rasor. [*Aside.*] Here is so much Sport going to be spoil'd, it makes me ready to weep again. A Pox o' this impertinent Lady *Fancyfull*, and her Plots, and her *French-woman* too; she's a whimsical, ill-natur'd Bitch, and when I have got my Bones broke in her Service, 'tis ten to one but my Recompence is a Clap; I hear them tittering without still. I'cod, I'll e'en go lug them both in by the Ears, and discover the Plot, to secure my Pardon.

[*Exit Rasor.*

Const. Pr'ythee, explain, *Heartfree.*

Heart. A fair Deliverance; thank my Stars and my Friend.

Bel. 'Tis well it went no farther; a base Fellow!

Lady Brute. What can be the meaning of all this?

Bel. What's his Meaning, I don't know; but mine is, that if I had married him——I had had no Husband.

Heart. And what's her Meaning I don't know; but mine is, that if I had married her—I had had Wife enough.

Sir John. Your People of Wit have got such cramp ways of expressing themselves, they seldom comprehend one another. Pox take you both, will you speak that you may be understood!

Enter Rasor *in sackcloth, pulling in* Lady Fancyfull and Madamoiselle.

Rasor. If they won't, here comes an Interpreter.

Lady Brute. Heavens! what have we here?

Rasor. A Villain——but a repenting Villain. Stuff which Saints in all Ages have been made of.

All. Rasor!

Lady Brute. What means this sudden Metamorphose?

Rasor. Nothing, without my Pardon.

Lady Brute. What Pardon do you want?

Rasor. Imprimis, Your Ladyship's; for a damnable Lie made upon your spotless Virtue, and set to the Tune of *Spring-Garden*. [*To Sir John.*] Next, at my generous Master's Feet I bend, for interrupting his more noble Thoughts with Phantoms of disgraceful Cuckoldom. [*To Const.*] Thirdly, I to this Gentleman apply, for making him the Hero of my Romance. [*To Heart.*] Fourthly, your Pardon, noble Sir, I ask, for clandestinely marrying you, without either bidding of Banns, Bishop's Licence, Friends Consent——or your own Knowledge. [*To Bel.*] And, lastly, to my good young Lady's Clemency I come, for pretending the Corn was sow'd in the Ground, before ever the Plough had been in the Field.

Sir John. [*Aside.*] So that, after all, 'tis a moot point, whether I am a Cuckold or not.

Bel. Well, Sir, upon Condition you confess all, I'll pardon you myself, and try to obtain as much from the rest of the Company. But I must know, then, who 'tis has put you upon all this Mischief?

Rasor. Satan, and his Equipage; Woman tempted me, Lust weakened me——and so the Devil over-came me; as fell *Adam*, so fell I.

Bel. Then pray, Mr. *Adam*, will you make us acquainted with your *Eve*?

Rasor. [*To Madam.*] Unmask, for the Honour of *France*.

All. Madamoiselle!

Madam. Me ask ten tousand Pardon of all de good Company.

Sir John. Why, this Mystery thickens, instead of clearing up. [*To Rasor.*] You Son of a Whore, you, put us out of our Pain.

Rasor. One Moment brings Sunshine. [*Shewing Madam.*] 'Tis true, this is the Woman that tempted me, but this is the Serpent that tempted the Woman; and if my Prayers might be heard, her Punishment for so doing shou'd be like the Serpent's of old—[*Pulls off Lady Fancyfull's Mask.*] She should lie upon her Face all the Days of her Life.

All. Lady *Fancyfull!*

Bel. Impertinent!

Lady Brute. Ridiculous!

All. Ha! ha! ha! ha! ha!

Bel. I hope your Ladyship will give me leave to wish you Joy, since you have own'd your Marriage yourself—[*To Heart.*] I vow 'twas strangely wicked in you to think of another Wife, when you had one already so charming as her Ladyship.

All. Ha! ha! ha! ha! ha!

Lady Fan. [*Aside.*] Confusion seize 'em, as it seizes me!

Madam. *Que le Diable e toute ce Mauraut de* Rasor.

Bel. Your Ladyship seems disorder'd: A breeding Qualm, perhaps, Mr. *Heartfree*: Your Bottle of Hungary Water to your Lady. Why, Madam, he stands as unconcern'd, as if he were your Husband in earnest.

Lady Fan. Your Mirth's as nauseous as yourself. *Belinda,* you think you triumph over a Rival now: *Helas! ma pauvre fille.* Where'er I'm Rival, there's no Cause for Mirth. No, my poor Wretch, 'tis from another Principle I have acted. I knew that Thing there wou'd make so perverse a Husband, and you so impertinent a Wife, that left your mutual Plagues should make you both run mad, I charitably would have broke the Match. He! he! he! he! he!

> [*Exit, laughing affectedly, Madamoiselle following her.*

Madam. He! he! he! he! he!

All. Ha! ha! ha! ha! ha!

Sir John. [*Aside.*] Why, now, this Woman will be married to somebody, too.

Bel. Poor Creature! what a Passion she's in! But I forgive her.

Heart. Since you have so much Goodness for her, I hope you'll pardon my Offence, too, Madam.

Bel. There will be no great Difficulty in that, since I am guilty of an equal Fault.

Heart. Then Pardons being past on all sides, pray let's to Church to conclude the Day's Work.

Const. But before you go, let me treat you, pray, with a Song a new-married Lady made within this Week; it may be of use to you both.

SONG.

I.

When yielding first to *Damon's* Flame,

I sunk into his Arms;
He swore he'd ever be the same,
Then rifled all my Charms.
But fond of what he'd long desir'd,
Too greedy of his Prey,
My Shepherd's Flame, alas! Expir'd
Before the Verge of Day.

II.

My Innocence in Lovers Wars
Reproach'd his quick Defeat;
Confus'd, asham'd, and bath'd in Tears,
I mourn'd his cold Retreat.
At length, Ah Shepherdess! cry'd he,
Wou'd you my Fire renew,
Alas, you must retreat like me,
I'm lost if you pursue.

Heart. So, Madam; now had the Parson but done his Business——

Bel. You'd be half weary of your Bargain.

Heart. No, sure, I might dispense with one Night's Lodging.

Bel. I'm ready to try, Sir.

Heart. Then let's to Church: And if it be our Chance to disagree——

Bel. Take heed—the surly Husband's Fate you see.

[Exeunt omnes.

FINIS.

CPSIA information can be obtained
at www.ICGtesting.com
Printed in the USA
LVHW081440240619
622182LV00036B/1624/P

9 781985 297388